A human life – what is it wor

This is a question that P

in Leading Broken People. I l

for many years, and am gratef

of leading and caring for broken people. Our cities are filled with broken and damaged people whose lives are being destroyed by addiction, rejection, abuse and poverty. But in Paul's eyes, these rejects are diamonds in the rough. He sees with the eyes of Jesus beyond the brokenness and "worthlessness."

I believe that as you read Leading Broken People, the Holy Spirit will give you a heart of compassion and faith to believe that no one is beyond the saving reach of Christ. Paul and Vicky's life of sacrifice in reaching others is inspiring. They believe, like I do, that the lost and broken can be not just reformed, but transformed into a new creation by the blood of Jesus. Paul sees that a human life has ultimate value because Jesus saw value in us by dying as a perfect sacrifice for our sins to redeem us from the prison we were all in. This book will show you the beauty that can be found in brokenness and that beauty is the life of Jesus.

Nicky Cruz, author of *Run Baby Run*

Paul Lloyd is unique and amazing. Few people I've ever met are better equipped to speak into bringing the best out of formerly broken people. Read on and be inspired'

Andy Hawthorne OBE,
CEO and founder, The Message Trust

Paul Lloyd is the real deal. He is a world-class leader, preacher and now author. If you want a book about the theory of leadership go elsewhere but if you want one carved out of real life then this book is a must read.

Matt Bird, founder and CEO of
Cinnamon Network International

God is in the restoration and renewal business and one of his very best repair shops is called Victory Outreach. The Manchester UK branch is led by Paul and Vicky Lloyd who in the power of Jesus have taken smashed lives and lovingly, patiently and powerfully renewed and restored those the world gave up on years ago. Not only that, these left behind people now lead and restore others into their full potential in Christ. I can't think of anyone more qualified to write on the subject of leading broken people. Every pastor leads broken people to some degree or other, and it's one of the most difficult pastoral challenges you will have. Buy this book and get a masterclass in how to do it from an experienced repair shop manager!

Rev Roger Sutton, Baptist minister, director of Gather and Movement Day UK, and Movement.org global hub leader

I have known Paul Lloyd for over 20 years and have so admired his work at Victory Outreach. The title of the book is perfect because it's what he does day in and day out; leading broken people. And he inspires others to do the same. So many books are about the theory behind an idea, this book is full of the daily reality.

Debra Green OBE, founding director of ROC

"I have seen Paul and Vicky's work develop and grow over many years and the fruit is extraordinary. If you are seeking wisdom, understanding and knowledge on leading broken people you will find it here in this book. It is a must read!"

David King, director of Kingdom Voice Limited (Salford)

Brilliant! A unique and insightful book. A must read for anyone who wants to understand the journey out of brokenness.

Barry Woodward, author of *Once an Addict*

To Loz

Happy 40th Birthday

LEADING BROKEN PEOPLE

You're a warrior and the battles you fight now are for your broken's futures. You dared it — And you're winning...

Paul Lloyd

 EPH 6:10-18

Matador
9 Priory Business Park,
Wistow Road, Kibworth Beauchamp,
Leicestershire. LE8 0RX
Tel: 0116 279 2299
Email: books@troubador.co.uk
Web: www.troubador.co.uk/matador
Twitter: @matadorbooks

ISBN 978 1800460 027

British Library Cataloguing in Publication Data.
A catalogue record for this book is available from the British Library.

Printed and bound in the UK by TJ Books Limited, Padstow, Cornwall
Typeset in 11pt Adobe Garamond Pro by Troubador Publishing Ltd, Leicester, UK

Matador is an imprint of Troubador Publishing Ltd

This book is dedicated firstly to my saviour and lord Jesus Christ, and secondly to my family – my amazing wife, Vicky, who is my true soulmate, and Lilie and Tomas my children, who bring so much joy to my life.

I am who I am because of the love they have all given me…

FOREWORD

Sonny Arguinzoni, international pastor
and founder of Victory Outreach International

Throughout my many years of ministry, I have met many young men and women who were broken, hurting and rejected by society. However, I have also seen beyond their outer appearance great potential and I have said, "If only they would surrender their lives to God and give God a chance to perform His will in their life".

Paul Lloyd was one of those young men that put his life into God's hands. He was once broken and hurting, but when he yielded his life to God and became a born-again Christian, God gave him a compassion to reach others, that like him, needed to hear the Gospel message of Jesus Christ, especially those bound by drug addiction and gangsterism.

Paul Lloyd's life has been an example to those that knew him before Christ came into his life; to those who know him today, and I believe to those who are yet to meet him. Paul Lloyd has touched thousands with his life-changing testimony. The miracle of God's redemption is clearly seen in his life. Paul Lloyd is a treasure out of darkness, and is now a beacon to others.

Jesus Christ abides in the Lloyd residence; he is a devoted husband to his wife Vicky and a loving father to his children. God has taken a man hardened by sin and transformed him into a great family man.

Paul Lloyd, was once broken and not much good to himself, today he is a leader, and Pastor to men and women who themselves have been changed by the Grace of God.

As you read this book, you will be inspired and challenged to reach your potential in Christ. As Paul Lloyd has clearly stated it is not an academic book or theological treaties; it is in fact a book for all of us, it is a book about our transformation by the power of God.

God Bless you, enjoy the book.

THE "WHY"

"Why" is a powerful word.

We use it in a variety of ways – from a cry of pain and confusion to a place of enquiry and a thirst for understanding. I've used this word in both of these scenarios, and quite often haven't received a satisfactory answer. But one thing I know is that if you don't know why you're doing what you're doing, you'll never get the best out of it.

So "why" this book? The answer might not completely satisfy you, but it came about after a series of events that literally forced me to write it, dragging my feet and grumbling to myself. I'd always wanted to write but never felt I had it in me. It's funny how we can swing between overestimating ourselves and underestimating ourselves, and this was the latter season. But then I was challenged by several people in a short space of time to put down some of the things I'd been teaching and preaching about for over two decades as the senior pastor of a church called Victory Outreach Manchester. Another cheeky someone told me that I probably even had a couple of books in me, and qualified this by ensuring me that even a broken clock is right twice a day so not to worry. But what capped it was a dinner with my wife, Vicky, and a friend of ours called Matt Bird, the CEO of Cinnamon Network International. During the meal the topic got around to books and he asked me what type of book I'd write. I had some vague thoughts about my testimony of change or a story of planting a church in inner-city Salford, but he pressed me for a title. Seemingly out of nowhere, I blurted, "Leading Broken People". The others went quiet and I started to crumble, but then they both spoke and said they were intrigued and that it sounded great. So that's when this book pregnancy began.

But here's the "why". Why did that title come out of me? I think it's probably for a few reasons. Firstly, it's what I do, and it's been my reality for twenty plus years as a pastor in the worldwide ministry of Victory Outreach International, which traditionally focuses on inner cities and their challenges. It's become almost natural to work with broken people. I've come to the conclusion that it must be something I'm supposed to do, because I can't seem to get away from it. It would be so much easier to work with "normal", functional (even wealthy?) people – and we do have those in our church – but there are always the broken ones, lots of them, looking for help. Gang members and criminals, addicts of every type and those unfortunate people who have just hit hard times in life seem to come to my door in one condition, and then a great many of them find their condition changing for the better.

Then there are the hard lessons I've learned and the patterns that you see and convictions you arrive at about how to actually see lives transformed and not just maintained in their hopelessness. That's really what this book contains. It's not an academic book, although I love learning and have studied at higher levels of education, and it's not a medical or psychological manual. I haven't studied those disciplines and I honour those who have. I've pastored and lead many doctors and nurses and psychiatrists and the like, and I've followed their advice when things move in that direction. I've had food and fun with them, walked with some through medical school and the mad first few years of hospital reality. I've prayed with and for them, I've conducted their weddings and dedicated their children and laughed and cried with them. But I couldn't do what they do. So, I don't think it's that either. It's also not a theological treatise, although it contains what I believe to be biblical truths, and I am convinced that it is these truths that form the basis of real transformation in people's lives.

If anything, this is just a book containing some things I've learned that I've come to see actually work. But here's where it can get challenging. You see, I believe that broken people can change form. I believe in the possibility of transformation, especially in those areas of addiction and crime that I've mostly been led to focus on, and the fact is that not everyone else does, which in my opinion leaves far too many people stuck between freedom and a cage. So, I wanted to write something that can offer some practical help to the ones who want to serve the broken by believing that there's something more for them, and then be willing to lead them there. If I were to tell you that I've seen literally thousands and thousands of people transformed in my life, it wouldn't be a lie. I'm one of them… and if I can change, I believe that anyone can.

THE BROKENNESS REALITY
(IT'S NOT ALWAYS WHAT
YOU THINK IT IS)

Broken people are everywhere.

The problem is they don't all come in the same package. They're not all broken in the same way. They don't necessarily look the same or sound the same, or haven't necessarily had the same experiences. Some of them don't even realise for a long time that they're broken.

When we think of that word and apply it to our own lives there comes a tension due to the effect the word "broken" has on different people.

Some people, when they see something is broken, immediately think of replacing it. I'm sure that's not something we'd welcome happening to us.

Others simply avoid whatever it is. Once again, being shunned is not a great experience, is it? Some just accept the fact that it's broken, shrug their shoulders and move on. Worse, though, is sensing from others that there's no hope or help available for your condition.

But there are those who look at something broken and have a desire to do something to help fix it.

This last desire is a noble one, but to lead someone from a place of brokenness to a place of fulfilment of their actual potential is another thing entirely. It's not a convenient thing. When speaking of leadership, I'm sure that pretty much anybody can lead a broken person anywhere – as long as they stay broken. But to lead someone from a state of brokenness to the place of fulfilling their potential will take more commitment than most people are willing to give and often goes beyond a nine-to-five mentality, or a thirty-minute appointment. It's a journey of the heart, but one that still needs to be guided by the mind. When you get down to the bottom line, leading broken people in the right direction is always going to be a sacrifice. Leading broken people often takes place on the second mile, not just the first and this is a place that's sparsely populated.

So, what qualifies you to help someone who's hurting or lead someone who's broken? Do you necessarily have to have walked in their shoes? In my experience the simple answer to that is, "No!" You don't have to have been a heroin addict to reach and help one. Nor do you have to have been divorced to help someone get through one. The list goes on. What's important is that you start with the right motive, take the right steps and push for the right outcome. Keeping the outcome in mind is really important, especially when it looks like nothing is working out as you planned. Many times, I've seen noble-minded people get involved with the work of helping broken people, and be well rewarded for it financially, but achieve little in terms of transformation of the lives of the people they work with. Maybe it's because whenever the need for the right income outweighs the need for the right outcome, you're usually left with something vitally important missing from the equation. Sadly, that's usually the point when broken people get replaced for a more financially viable option and that response is too common for my liking.

I think that a large part of someone's response to brokenness is dependent on the value they place on the object. For instance, a broken glass can be easier to replace than to fix, even when it's yours. But a broken watch your father gave you is another thing altogether. Then there's the bit of broken pavement (sidewalk) that you try to avoid. Unless, of course, it's directly outside your house. Or how about when you walk past a place with a broken window and you see it, but there's nothing you can do about it, so you shrug your shoulders and walk on by? But what about if it was your window that was broken? Would you leave it in that condition?

Perceptions and values seem to change when you have a sense of ownership towards the broken thing, and this is what will enable you to continue when things get challenging. On the subject of "ownership", though, it's essential to remember that it's the mission you're taking ownership of, not the person. We don't want co-dependency or weird, controlling relationships to develop. What we're looking for is a sense of commitment to seeing things through. There's a big difference between having the right boundaries and erecting the walls of a prison around someone you're working with.

IRREPLACEABLE
(WHAT PEOPLE ARE WORTH)

Here's a question that can help you to focus on the importance of working towards helping hurting or broken people – what is a life really worth? How much would you be willing to pay?

I've found that many people, when asked this question, treat it in an abstract kind of way, but when it's personalised it takes on a different urgency. So, let me put it this way – what's *your* life worth?

Most people would agree with the idea that life is valuable, but then they struggle with the question of exactly how much a life is worth. Economists and insurance specialists, and even medical professionals, have their own ways of weighing the worth of a human life, and if we're honest so do we all, but the question remains – what are people really worth?

When you can answer that question with conviction to yourself, you will find it will either release you to help others or restrain you from helping others. For example, if you have a low view of life – if you think that people are just a type of computer-controlled robots in "meat suits" – then it's likely you won't necessarily expend much energy in helping someone who looks like he or she has been irreparably broken. If they're mentally broken or messed up on drugs or alcohol, or even physically damaged in some way, it seems to be the case that whenever there is a low view of a person's worth, not much will be done for them. At best they will be maintained, but never believed that they can ever change or be transformed into something better.

I was once told that, "Once a junkie, always a junkie…" As a former long-term heroin addict, I was placed on a lifetime maintenance program of methadone (which is a pharmaceutical heroin substitute). The common belief around addiction is that "junkies" can't change. At best, it's thought to be a disease or a mental illness, and at worst, it's a self-inflicted form of destruction with the "junkie" deserving everything they get. I can understand people feeling uncomfortable with addiction because addicts can be unpredictable, their lives are messy and dealing with them can take a lot of effort. But when you see their actual worth as a human, you'll put that effort in because you'll see it more as an investment than a sacrifice. This is especially true when the addict is one of your family… but even if they're not part of your family, they are part of someone's family and are valuable to them.

When you have a high view on life and its worth, you will pull out all the stops to ensure that broken people are not just cast away or forgotten about.

THE THREE TYPES OF BROKENNESS

So, how can you know what type of brokenness is facing you? There are three main ones that can be understood using the illustration of an item that the majority of us have – a mobile phone.

Have you ever had that sinking feeling when you've dropped your phone and you pick it up and the screen is shattered? You can see it's broken straight away, and you know immediately that it's going to be very difficult to use it properly now. It could even cause you harm because of what's obviously wrong with it. But I've also had it happen to me where I've dropped my phone and picked it up and the screen was fine! What a massive relief, right? The screen was okay, the case was okay… but it wouldn't work! While the outside looked okay, something had broken on the inside – something I couldn't see or even get to. Sometimes that's even worse than having a broken screen. The only way forward in this scenario is to get expert help. Then there's the time you go to use your phone and… nothing! No connection!

The outside is intact, the inside is fine and everything seems like it's working, but the connection is broken. It's usually something that you don't have the power to change but the effect is the same – something is broken and we all know the feelings of powerlessness and frustration that come with it. Let's look at these examples more closely:

Outer brokenness

This type of brokenness is usually obvious. Moving from mobile phones to humans, this could be a physical problem, or maybe even a disability. These can be genetically inherited or have come about through sickness or an accident, but they can be seen – and the fact is that when you can see brokenness, you can generally handle it better. In my church there is a young man that I saw grow up with severe cerebral palsy. He was born with the condition and because it was obvious, everyone treated him accordingly and were quick to help him, because it could be seen that he couldn't do certain things for himself.

Then there's my wife, Vicky. At the age of forty, in 2011, she was diagnosed with bone cancer in her left leg. parosteal osteosarcoma, to be exact. The rare tumour was measured at 23cm from femur to ankle and the first response by her consultant was amputation. But after a series of what can only be viewed as "miraculous" events (as actually quoted by her surgical consultant), she ended up having the tumour removed, along with her fibula, tibia and knee. These bones were then replaced with a made-to-measure, silver-coated titanium prosthetic implant, which incorporated a new knee. While she retained her leg, she became physically disabled, needing to learn to walk again. She has a single working nerve and a permanent drop foot, and due to the margins needed when removing the tumour, much of her muscle is gone. Her life, and that of our little family was irrevocably changed because of it. This presents another nuance to the outer brokenness scenario, because most of the time her leg is covered and so can't be readily seen. Her limp can be missed and the different shape of her leg can be hidden, and so she can be thought to be in perfect working order. It's only when people see the reality that their mindsets change. The help required for Vicky was originally focused on getting her physically "fixed", but when that was done as best as could be expected her need changed. She then needed to be guided towards and allowed to believe the possibility that she was still valuable and there was a viable future for her. Thankfully, she embraced the opportunities and is now back functioning as a mum and a church leader in her own right. She's a powerful communicator and speaks at conferences all over the world, even sharing the story of her comeback from that setback and giving hope to others through her testimony. Vicky will be the first to tell you that it was, in large part, due to people who refused to write her off and replace her that she is able to be in the place she is today.

You can be one of those people in someone else's life. The thing, though, with outer brokenness is that people help because it's obvious – you can literally see what needs doing, and if you're the type of person who has the conviction that brokenness is redeemable and not just replaceable, you can actually play a major part in seeing the broken pieces put back together. In fact, you can even bring improvement to the situation and not just maintenance.

I had a revelation of this when I saw an example of a Japanese art form called "*kintsugi*", which translates as "golden joinery". The artist takes a piece of pottery with a crack in it and uses a lacquer, which is dusted with a precious metal such as gold, silver or platinum, to fill and repair the defect. The crack is not hidden but highlighted, and the thinking behind this is that when treated in the right way, a defect can actually become a beautiful feature. The pot or vase was originally valuable, with time and effort going into its formation, and so even though it had suffered a setback, it could be redeemed, and in fact after its treatment it actually becomes more valuable. How great is that?

This has been my personal experience since I began following Jesus Christ. Everyone has cracks and flaws and defects, but none of them faze God as He became one of us and fully understands the fragility of humanity. Cracks may appear in our lives, but the beauty of humanity in its originally intended form is still at the centre of God's will for us. In fact, there's even something better in store for humans in eternity. This is the biblical narrative of redemption, where broken humans are added to by the life of the creator God in Christ and made new, and that narrative is ongoing, and we can be part of it.

This all means the work of repair in a person's life can even become a testimony of hope and healing to others, and by removing the shame and stigma associated with that broken piece we can enable that person to realise how valuable they truly are. What defines us are not our past mistakes or experiences, but our present decisions that begin the work of birthing a new future reality. And we are worth more than we could ever know. So, don't write off anyone just because of their outer challenges. If you simply add the precious metal of belief and opportunity to their broken pieces, you will help them to become the beautiful people they were created to be.

With these outer casing situations, it can seem simpler to help because they can be seen. It's obvious, right? But what happens when the brokenness is not obvious?

Inner brokenness

This type of brokenness is not always obvious because what can't be seen can be dismissed or simply not understood.

Mental illness and emotional problems can fit into this category. It's really sad how, because these conditions can't be seen, many people ignore them, or even worse, don't believe that anything is really wrong. This way of thinking can keep the broken person in an often-painful place of unfulfilled potential.

In the distant past, people with these inner problems were often sentenced to lunatic asylums or ostracised by "normal" society. (I've often wondered what people mean when they use the term "normal". If it's what I suspect, I tried being "normal" once and it was the worst two minutes of my life…) We live today, however, in a new world of discovery, where these challenges are more readily recognised and accepted and can even be overcome, so that they don't have to hinder the potential of the sufferer.

Identifying the cause is the first step to helping in this situation, and as a Christian, I've experienced three particular mindsets regarding the causes of inner brokenness:

The first goes something like: "It's caused by a failure to obey or practise what the word of God says", and is a normal response by many in Churches. So therefore, it's self-inflicted and basically just sinful behaviour. Their answer then is for you to start doing things "God's way" again and all will be fine. While this is a possibility in some cases, and putting the practicalities of the Bible into action can and does have an effect, it's not the only reason for inner turmoil. It's just the first "go-to" point for many Christians. What happens, though, when you're doing everything you know you should be doing but still have a period where depression covers you like a shroud? Maybe there's another reason? When you read the Bible and see people like Job suffering it gives you another insight. How about Elijah, who wanted to die right after experiencing a spiritual high? Then there's David, who experienced the dark side of life many times. You just have to read his psalms to get an understanding of this reality. So, maybe throwing a quick judgement on the problem is not always the way to go?

The second mindset I've come across – which can be disturbing if not understood, and sometimes even when it is – is that the mental or emotional problem is demonic in origin. To secularly minded people this is pure nonsense and not worth even entertaining. But I have come across actual cases like this and the Bible definitely speaks about these things. I've also had some weird experiences myself. In these cases, I've seen the power of faith and prayer literally setting someone free. However, to simply assume this position without regard for any other evidence is unhelpful and can even be dangerous. It's also true that condemning it without investigating it is also potentially dangerous. In my opinion, cases like this are not as common as some would maintain, but also not as rare as some would like to believe, so clear and careful handling of this is really important.

The third mindset is that there's some form of physiological problem. Maybe there's a chemical deficiency somewhere or a breakdown in a thought process? This moves the problem from the realm of what could be termed "super-spirituality" into a place of a reality that is still spiritual but more practical, and I think this is more usually the case. And where this is the case, medication can be a viable option. But care should be taken here that medication is not the only option offered. By far the most people suffering from inner brokenness need counselling, not medication, and worryingly that's not the first thing given by medical professionals. Due to the time constraints placed on doctors and the pressure from the giant pharmaceutical companies, it's no surprise that a pill is more convenient to give than a listening ear or a shoulder to cry on.

Back to the mobile phone analogy – if the screen is broken it can seem like a simple fix, but when the inside is broken it's usually best to get some expert help. So, take the problem to someone who knows more about it than you do. If it's a spiritual problem, get help from someone equipped for that, a pastor or minister, and if it's a physiological problem, seek out a doctor or psychiatrist or psychologist. Where it looks as if talking might help, get a qualified counsellor to come on board to take the broken person where they need to go. By all means be available to the broken one, but don't try to go beyond your remit. Expert help is the way forward and when the wellbeing of the broken person you're working with is at the front of your decision making, this will flow naturally. My wife and I, as church pastors, will at times outsource people to experts in other disciplines. It's okay to do this and can actually speed up the recovery process. The truth is, it doesn't matter who gets the credit as long as the person you're working with gets better. Right?

None of these solutions works well, though, without the right connections.

Broken connection

Connections are vital for achieving the outcomes that we believe are at the core of our existence. We all have a main purpose to our lives, but quite often that gets lost in the chaos and confusion of the society we live in.

In the context of the mobile phone analogy, the outer case is intact and everything is working, but you can't get a signal. There's no connection to the provider. Somehow it was broken, and if it can't be restored you could end up with a good-looking, functional phone that's not fit for its purpose. If you can't use it for what it was intended for, then what a waste. Therefore, this is the part that completes the restoration purpose.

In my opinion, everyone starts off like this, with a broken connection. Don't get me wrong, on a purely physical level there are many connections that offer themselves to us, from parental connections at the beginning of life to friends and mentors that we connect with throughout our lives, and all of these are important. Whenever people are disconnected from these fulfilling relationships there will always be a lack, and it's really important that at the right time these connections are looked at and strengthened. Many times, we have assisted the people we're working with to reattach with someone relationally. It's also important to connect them to the right people that can help them to make progress, and this is an area that takes work but also brings fulfilment. It's always better to be insulated than isolated.

I don't think it stops with these types of connections, though. Physically, someone can be complete, and mentally and emotionally they can be fully functioning – but how are they spiritually? To many people raised with a secular worldview where all that matters is time, space and matter, this question can seem irrelevant or even comical. But is it? What if there is a creator and He created everything with purpose so that you can live in that creation with a meaning that goes beyond just the things that can be seen, heard, felt, smelled or tasted? What if that connection was broken through choices? That's the scenario the Bible describes as sin. Sin occurs when someone makes a choice where the creator God who provides the ultimate connection is replaced by self-will. When you take the path of wanting to judge and decide things according to your own wants and desires – and act upon that decision – you break connection with God. I know it's stretching the phone analogy a bit thin, but if you decide you don't want to fulfil the terms of your contract with your network provider you will be disconnected. Then you have a phone that can appear to be okay but essentially is not fit to do what it was created to do.

However, the good news is that the provider of true reality can be reconnected to. That is the view of Christianity, in that the spiritual brokenness that is common to all can be fixed through the work of Christ. He formed the connection back to God the father, because He paid the ultimate price of giving His life to settle the debt that we owed.

When all these areas of brokenness are understood, there is more chance of being able to concentrate your efforts in the most effective places to help people live the amazing and valuable lives they were created to live.

So, don't replace broken people – add gold and watch them increase in value and begin to shine like never before. Each one you help is a treasure taken out of darkness and every one of them is worth it.

THE POWER OF ONE (TRANSFORMED PEOPLE TRANSFORM THINGS)

Never overlook the power of one.

Don't forget that even though there are so many broken people out there and helping them is hard, when you just help the one in front of you it can have a domino effect, and by helping that one in front of you it can set a miracle in motion.

For a while now, the subject of transformation has been a hot topic. Debates and conferences and articles by experts and commentators have pointed people towards the ideal of city and community change. I've been to quite a few of these conferences because I believe in transformation, but to me, it's more than just a trendy topic, or even an incredible ideal – it's a necessary and expected part of my faith and work as a pastor. And while it's true that in order for us to see our cities and societies transformed it will take lots of differently skilled people working together strategically, the simple fact is that it can begin very practically with individual people, because transformed people tend to transform their environment.

Take me for instance. I committed crime and sold drugs to people who committed crime to buy drugs to feed their habit. It was a self-perpetuating and ongoing cycle of destruction. But when my life was transformed, part of that cycle stopped, and in fact started going in the opposite direction. I began to help other people to stop taking drugs, which meant that they didn't need to commit crime to get money to fund their habit. That in turn had a knock-on effect in terms of insurance, the use of health services, a reduction in the pressure on police forces and court proceedings and prison staff. Families and children were positively affected, and that takes pressure off the social services. Added to that, the peace of mind you get from not having to worry if you're going to be robbed or burgled, or your child is going to end up as a statistic in a file somewhere, and you can begin to see the scope of this work.

Imagine that one life then reaches and helps ten others who do the same. In a couple of transformation cycles you've seen a hundred lives changed for the better – all from one transformed life.

I think, though, that there is can be a misunderstanding of the difference between "reformed" and "transformed". Even though you might think it's just semantics and different words being used, they are actually two different concepts entirely.

"Reformation" means making changes to something (or someone) with the intention of setting it back on the right path. This concept is okay, but in my ministry, to people struggling with substance misuse, I've seen far too many addicts "reformed" for a little while and then falling right back onto the addiction treadmill. The mistake is in expecting that the path they were on before they became addicted was a better one. But let's face it – that path led to them becoming an addict, so why would you want someone to go back to that?

Sadly, there are many so-called "experts" who are of the opinion, "Once an addict – always an addict!" The best they see for addicts is that they can be "junkies without a habit" or "dry drunks", or, in other words, that addicts will never be completely free. They can be reformed but not transformed and to me, this only has the potential for a seesaw existence of getting "straight" only to walk straight back into the same patterns as before.

But "transformation" is a different concept. Transformation is explained as "the act or process of changing completely: a complete change".

The end result of transformation in the life of an addict is a life where addiction is just a horrible memory, not a continued and constant presence of temptation. The key is that with this, you're directing that person towards a different future, not trying to get them back to a place where they were before addiction.

A reformed life comes through *lifestyle change*, but a transformed life comes from a *life exchange*. In Christianity, it works like this – you give Jesus your wrongs, and He gives you His rights…

This is what makes the major difference between "reform" and "transform". Reformation leaves us much the way we were in our old being with some minor, but perhaps significant, changes. Transformation changes us into a very new being, with major shifts in our lifestyles, relationships and life focus. While it's true that some return to addiction, the vast majority of those who have experienced a life transformation continue to live free.

Let's look at the Bible for a moment to see how Jesus went about transforming cities and societies by transforming people. There are two places that clearly benefited from this "one transformed life" thing – Samaria and Gadara.

The first example is a story about a hurting woman who comes into direct contact with Jesus at a well near a town called Samaria, sometime in the early first century ad. It's amazing how the problems she is struggling with translate into our own modern day and age. When you read through the account in John's gospel in chapter 4:1–42, three really important things stand out that highlight how Jesus works with people in order to facilitate transformation. These processes are also mirrored when Jesus comes into contact with a man with serious spiritual and psychological issues in Mark's gospel, chapter 5:1–20.

It's important to see that these simple processes can work in different scenarios. The first example is a woman with severe relationship problems. These had caused her to become isolated and on top of that, she had some faulty religious concepts that also included some cultural bias. Don't be surprised to come across people in our modern-day society, and even churches, that look like this. Relational breakdown is a huge issue and can literally break someone's world in to pieces.

The second one is a man who had terrorised his neighbourhood. He was violent and a self-harmer, who everyone was afraid of and couldn't do anything to help him except isolate him and restrain him. Once again, this is not an uncommon problem in society. The fact he was possessed by evil spirits is an unusual one and not something you'll always come up against, but in fact can be a much simpler fix than some other mental and emotional problems we face in our society.

So, what did Jesus do that we can learn from and implement?

1) He met them where they were at

This is incredibly important if you are going to see anything positive take place in someone's life. Going into someone's reality is one of the most powerful steps we can take. Jesus did that by entering His own creation and becoming a part of it as a human baby in order to reach us where we are at.

Jesus didn't expect everyone to be changed before he'd do anything for them, and in some cases, this is what some "helpers" of hurting people tend to want to see. Instead, He presented Himself in our reality, and by doing that we have something unique – a knowable God.

For the couple we're looking at, that meant physically being with them and this is a powerful expression of intent. Whenever you do that you show that you care about that person before that person will start to care about whatever you know could help them.

In terms of working with broken people, this personal touch is one of the main starting blocks on their journey of transformation.

There are various ways we can do this, including street-level intervention or personal visitation to homes or hostels, hospitals and prison cells.

I will add that if you're going to do the street work, it's best you don't go alone – I'm born-again but I wasn't born-again yesterday! Use wisdom and have backup where necessary, but go wherever you need to go. It's really important that we meet people where they're at and then be present in their reality, at least for a while, so we can then begin to help lift them up out of it. That's what Jesus models and it works if you work it.

2) He confronted them with reality

Jesus immediately saw their problems. The woman had relational issues and the man had emotional and mental challenges (caused by being literally possessed by demons! I've encountered this in reality as a missionary in India, Israel and the Middle East. But I've also come across it in the UK – London, in fact. This is very different from just a chemical imbalance or an emotional trauma. I understand this is a difficult thing to come to terms with, but in my opinion – from biblical study and experience – it's rare but real). There were times that people came to Jesus with their problems but in this case, He entered their reality. When you do that, you can then get a good look at it.

You can generally see pretty quickly what that reality looks like, but maybe they can't. Maybe they've become blinded to their condition and have adapted to it in such a way that it's become their "normal". Or maybe they have run out of the energy needed to try to change their situation. This can happen when circumstances knock someone back again and again.

When working with addiction, for example, the first hurdle to overcome is not necessarily denial of the condition – addicts generally know they have a problem. The key thing to overcome is the denial about the consequences of their condition. The fact that their health won't stand up to much more, or their family can't handle much more, or that their future will be irreparably ripped apart are some of the very real consequences of staying in that lifestyle and need to be taken seriously.

With other types of brokenness, it can be more subtle or more specific. For example, I've come across many people in denial of a mental issue, even though it's glaringly obvious to everyone around them, so they refuse any treatment. This makes offering a solution difficult. So, the work here is to help them see their reality. And how about the person who has a life that's seemingly successful, but whose marriage is breaking apart? These things will need to be addressed, and this takes both sensitivity and courage to do it right.

When you have fresh eyes and an objective perspective, you have the power to begin the process of helping them make the right adjustments. It's a little like having twenty-twenty vision and walking into the house of someone whose eyesight is compromised. You can see what they miss. That's what Jesus modelled and when we follow His example in confronting the problem, we can become a big part in enabling positive solutions.

3) He presented them with a solution

The key is to present the truth in a way that they'll understand, and one of the best ways to do this is to show them how different the possibilities are from the reality they know. Ask questions where necessary and listen to what they tell you, but when it's time to talk use direct language.

I've found that footprints can often be better than signposts where solutions are concerned. What I mean is that people who have successfully overcome something similar to the person you're working with can often be the catalyst needed to encourage them to make the changes they need to make, rather than just offering them data or information. Real-life testimonies are powerful things where transformation is concerned so that the person you're working with can begin to see not only what's necessary, but also what's possible.

When I work in prisons, I'll take ex-prisoners to testify. When you're working with addicts, ex-addicts can be the catalyst. You get the point? But don't limit yourself to just trying to get people out of a lifestyle. Many times, I've seen that offering a view of a life that's being desired can also really help someone make a change. My wife, Vicky, was helped whilst in her addiction to look towards a different life by a nurse and some "straight-going" Christians who gave her a glimpse of a different future.

Then there's the really practical stuff – housing or further education, so they can move out of their old cycle. My friend Simon Edwards, in Stoke, began "The Walk" project when he came out of prison. It started by reaching and helping men as they were released and providing them with housing and support. I was able to help in a small way at the beginning with some resources and experience and I've also signposted men there. Today it's flying, with not only housing available but also work for the men and even a rehab called "Liberty Farm". Amazing transformations take place through this charity.

Another friend, Andy Hawthorne, founder of "The Message" in Manchester, opened an enterprise centre to facilitate the same type of thing happening, and I've sent men and women there after they've completed our programme, to further their freedom by exposing them to new spheres of employment. My organisation, Victory Outreach, has always tried to provide onward solutions. We see people moving into further education, employment and their own housing, and some even go on to become ministers of religion, pastoring their own churches, and whatever we can't provide, we will signpost people to the places that can help them grow forward. The African saying that "it's a village that brings up a child" rings true where helping hurting people is concerned. The next point, though, is crucial and sometimes not really believed.

4) He expected a positive outcome

This is probably the most crucial part of the process. Even though it's been placed last, it should actually be the thing at the front of your mind when setting out to work with broken people, so try to start with the end in mind.

Sadly, I've found that most people settle for maintenance. Stopping people becoming worse is a good beginning, but in my opinion, if that's the only outcome you're looking forward to it's not enough. This point is one that probably causes the most friction between people who engage in helping broken people. Some will tell you that people can't fundamentally change – just as a leopard can't change its spots. They'll tell you that "once a junkie, always a junkie". They'll say things like, "you're always in recovery," but that's not been my experience. And it's definitely not the outcome that Jesus expects. I'm not just an ex-addict. Neither is my wife, or thousands of others who have been transformed from all sorts of broken lifestyles. The outcome that should be expected is transformation – fundamental life change. Anything less is shooting too low.

THE PATHFINDER
(CHALLENGES TO CHANGE)

Change is good. Tell yourself that as often as is necessary.

One day, hopefully, you'll be standing in the future that you somehow knew was on its way into your life, but wouldn't it be great if you could stand there looking back on the past and see how much you've changed and how much difference your life has made to others?

In his book *Pathfinder*, about his experiences as an officer in the British army Parachute Regiment's Pathfinder platoon, David Blakeley speaks about the role of his unit within the British army. This unit (PF platoon) specialises in advance reconnaissance missions, often deep behind enemy lines, where they mark out drop zones (DZs) and helicopter landing sites (HLSs) for use by the units that would be following them into action. As you can imagine, being an elite unit with an incredibly demanding selection process, there's not many of them. If you'll flow with me here, I think that too often we think that those "warriors" who help hurting people in our churches and society to change are the same type of thing – an elite force of specialists. But the truth is that, while the army Pathfinders definitely are that and more, in our context the qualification for helping people to change is that you've changed in some area yourself. Obviously, it helps to increase your skill and knowledge base, but you don't have to wait until you're some kind of "expert" before extending a helping hand to a needy person.

On this point, Captain Blakeley interestingly recounts how his unit used a particular saying a lot. Possibly originating with Sir Winston Churchill, it simply says:

"Shake change by the hand, before change grips you by the throat".

This quote sums up the attitude that you need when the prospect of change is part of the equation you're facing. And the fact is that change is always going to be a major part of life because everything changes. So, you either make change your friend, or one day it's going to treat you like an enemy. Or, in other words, everything changes but not all changes are positive. If you're passive about change you might find change overtaking you in ways that you really don't want, so it's best to be intentional about changing.

Unfortunately, change isn't the easiest thing in the world to actually do and one of the main reasons why people don't enjoy it is because it's uncomfortable.

There's another great book by Bruce Wilkinson called *The Dream Giver*, which begins like this:

"Not long ago and not far away a Nobody called Ordinary lived in the Land of Familiar…"

The book is about how to identify and overcome the obstacles that keep millions from living the life they were created for and it takes this person called "Ordinary" on a journey of change. On this journey, Ordinary had lots of decisions to make as he made his way closer to his big dream – he made hard choices, he made difficult changes, and he even made big sacrifices. He saw how pursuing his dream could cause him a lot of discomfort and that he would have to do unusual things in unusual places… and he realised that to do what he most loved, he'd have to do what he most dreaded.

Then he saw it clearly – he could either keep his comfort and stay a Nobody, or he could keep his dream and become a Somebody; but to do that he had to leave the Land of Familiar.

So, Ordinary left the comfort zone and went through the wasteland following a being called "Faith", and found just enough to drink, and ate fruit that wasn't sweet and wasn't sour but was satisfying…

I think this pretty much sums up most of us, if we're really honest. We want to be somebody and do something important or memorable, but to actually see something like that come to pass we have to be prepared to change. At first there's usually some resistance which needs to be overcome, because if we're honest, at some level of our being we fear it and what it brings with it.

This resistance to the process of change is mainly because of 2 main things:

A sense of loss

People emotionally feel a sense of loss in the process of change. Have you ever felt like you were losing or had lost something? How did you react? Didn't you try to hold on to whatever you were losing?

I call this "The Pitbull's bone principle".

When I was seventeen, I got a Pitbull puppy. They were rare in the UK in those days and I had the most fun raising him. His name was Danny Boy and he became my constant companion. Contrary to popular opinion, this breed of dog is the most loyal and intelligent dog you can hope to have, and although a bit boisterous to be sure, when exercised well they are extremely chilled out, loveable and fun to have. I do agree that not everyone should have one, but I hope you're getting the picture that they're not all "devil dogs" as some would have it. Anyway, Danny never bit me (except playfully by accident when I would wrestle him – and even then, he'd thankfully hold back his full bite). He was extremely well-trained and obedient because I was intentional about doing that, and one thing he loved more than anything is when I would get him a huge, juicy beef bone as a reward for something good he'd done from the local butcher. This would be sawed in two and would be full of delicious (to a dog at least) bone marrow. Danny would lay contentedly chewing on that bone for days. There would come a time when it would be done, but he'd bury it and dig it back up and go at it again. Whenever it was time to give it up, he found it the most difficult thing to do. He would not give that stinking thing up willingly. He'd growl menacingly and even show his teeth in a menacing way. He couldn't help it – and neither can we when this happens to us.

It's just a natural, and sometimes desperate, emotion to hold on to what you know. Like the bone scenario, what was once a good thing might not be good anymore and I've seen people get stuck in a place that's now stopped being good.

Even destructive things like bad relationships or addictions or negative habits can seem better than an unknown alternative. Whether we realise it or not, we can't face the seeming loss involved. There's a loss of power and control at first. Then it seems as if there's a loss of familiarity or unconscious tradition or ritual. This causes a loss of comfort and eventually a loss of stability, and the feeling of loss is an empty feeling in the pit of the stomach – it's a punch to the heart; it's like something grips you by the throat to choke you and then the panic kicks in.

It doesn't even matter if people know that the change is needed because they feel they may be losing something in the change, and so it causes them to resist the change. And it's because these emotions are based on some elements of truth that it's so hard because it means that things are going to be different in some way. And that leads to the other biggie where change is concerned:

A sense of fear

If we're honest, most of us in some way fear the unknown. But fear is a terrible enemy to give in to, because it has no mercy. Even if you surrender to it, it will still keep strangling you until there is no life left in you, and it's this aspect of change that causes far too many people to just settle for staying the same. Because, when things change, priorities shift, schedules are altered and commitments are looked at. These adjustments then cause anxiety because they require people to do things differently, and nothing is so secure as the familiar. It's comforting and probably not challenging, which is why most of us avoid change at all costs.

But, by avoiding change, we create even bigger problems, such as lost opportunities, broken relationships, or sometimes even a completely wasted life. I've seen this too many times, where someone has incredible potential but resists changing something or somewhere and sadly ends up as a "could've been" … living in the land of regret.

So, what can we do to help someone in this situation? Let's go back to my Pitbull.

The first advantage I had was that I had a relationship with Danny Boy. He trusted me. This aspect of relationship can never be highlighted enough for someone in a leadership capacity.

The old saying, "They don't care how much you know until they know how much you care", is a true one. And this doesn't have to be a huge undertaking – just paying them some attention, listening and giving some time to them is really all it takes, as long as it's sincere. But the next part was the clincher; I didn't just ask him to give up his old bone – I gave him an alternative… I showed him the new bone, all fresh and juicy. After a few growls and a few sniffs, the loss of the old was offset by the potential of the new. And then I'd stroke him and show him love and tell him, "Good boy, well done…"

Practically, we can do this in two ways:

1) My story… your story - sharing your own testimony of change

I'm a firm believer that "footprints are better than signposts" when leading some kind of change. If you're offering an alternative to something that needs to go it's important to show something real, and quite often your own experiences can paint a workable picture for someone else. One of the best ways of doing this is by telling your story – how change happened in your life. This is really important because of how the human brain works.

When you tell your story it often helps to begin with the problem or challenge you faced, which introduces a certain tension to the story, and because of this tension your body produces the hormone cortisol. This releases adrenaline when the tension is experienced and biologically makes people tune in to what you're saying. Add to this some personal details and this causes a sense of empathy, and so the bonding chemical, oxytocin, is released. Oxytocin and cortisol are powerful together, and as you tell your story this brings the moment called, by people who study this stuff (especially film makers and advertisers), "transportation". Your brain then begins to think that it is actually happening right now, and it feels like you've become part of the story yourself. This is why we cry, or laugh, or whatever, as we watch a good film and is a form of what's known as "neural coupling". Suddenly, you can see the alternative being presented as a real option and you find yourself actively involved in the story.

But the key to a strong story is "resolution". Resolution is the point where you come to a decision that something needs to be done and there's a determination to actually do something about it.

With resolution, dopamine is released. This is the "feel-good" chemical and is designed to reward us when we've overcome something difficult. So, when you show how a change you were facing was overcome, it's a bit like when my old dog, Danny Boy, realised that there was something better than his old, dirty, stinking wreck of a bone that was available to him. The loss is still the same, but now it becomes more of an investment and not just a sacrifice, because you can see that whatever you give up in order to change is making room for something better.

That's the power of a story. Personal stories demonstrate relevance by making truth more accessible, and that's why they have such an amazing impact. Just don't forget that the other person is not looking for you to be some kind of hero to them. People undergoing change are not looking for the hero of your story, they are looking for a guide – a pathfinder – someone who's already been there – to help them become the hero of their own story. I believe the desired outcome to an engaging story is that the hearer is going to be different by the end of it.

There is another thing that's needed which is just as

important as your personal story, and it's your ongoing, personal presence.

2) Be there - don't disengage when they engage

The second practical thing you can do is to journey with them, at least until they're safely on their way. I've found that the best leaders are those who are continually embracing change in some form or other, and because they're in constant motion, making progress in the right direction in their own lives, it's easier for them to journey with someone else who's also beginning to engage in that process.

Your presence becomes important because of the other main enemy of change – fear – which tries to come creeping back into the process of change, saying things like, "You're not good enough," or, "You're not going to make it," and so this is where your continuing and truly engaged love for the person you're helping is crucial.

I find that John the apostle understood this concept better than almost anyone else I've ever read. When speaking to a group of early followers of Christ, he talks to them about love, and how in its pure form love is unconditional and not just a response to something good, but an attitude of life which reflects the nature of the creator God, and how love is the antidote to fear:

There is no fear in love, but perfect love casts out fear. For fear has to do with punishment, and whoever fears has not been perfected in love.

1 JOHN 4:18 (ESV)

This "perfect" love, which in context means mature or complete, leaves no room for fear to control a person's life and your ongoing, unconditional relationship with the one you're helping to develop does that as you journey with them, reminding them that the changes they're going through are not a punishment but an investment in a better future. There will come times when they want to give up on the whole process, declaring, "It's too hard!" Then your role is to remind them that being unhappy and unfulfilled is hard and changing is hard, and then help them choose the type of "hard" they want to live – a positive hard or a negative hard. Your role at that point is to help them stay on track until they enter the phase where changing into something or someone new becomes a positive habit. This can take thirty days or more to become set in their experience, so be prepared for a journey of that length. But then, all of a sudden, just like a child learning to ride a bike, they won't need you to hold them up anymore as they wobble off under their own steam. Their journey then becomes about continued practice, because although practice doesn't actually make perfect, it does make what you're doing more permanent.

You then move from being someone who directly shows others the path forward and helps them find stability and security on the path, to making sure they stick to the path.

The relationship progresses from direct mentorship to a more distanced accountability. You've been through those phases yourself and already know that the journey leads somewhere good, and by using your experience in this manner you open the way for others to benefit. In this way, you become a leader because you have people following you, not just a lone scout who has just reached somewhere before anyone else.

So, be a pathfinder, because pathfinders lead the way.

Make your mark and leave some tracks for others to benefit from. Have change as your friend... and then introduce that friendly change to someone else... because change is good.

THE LIMIT BREAKER (SMASHING GLASS CEILINGS)

Most people limit themselves in some way.

It's almost as if they have a barrier to their potential – a little bit like a lid on a jar – that stops them from becoming the person they were created to become. They may be able to see the possibility – it could be in touching distance – but like a starving man on the wrong side of a bakery window, they just can't seem to get through it to get the good stuff.

I once heard the term "glass ceiling" used to describe this phenomenon. Glass ceilings are those annoying things that let you see where you want to go, but stop you from actually getting there. The term was originally used in the late 1970s to explain the difficulties that women had in the workplace, but my observation of people that are trying to step forward from a place of brokenness is that this frustration is common to them also, whatever their gender. A lot of people get really close to their purpose and bounce off something that they can't even see – an invisible barrier. When this happens, they become "capped" or limited. If you want to help someone to become everything they were created to become, then these glass ceilings need to be smashed. The challenge is to not become what's called an "enabler". This is a person that can actually "love someone to death", by trying to do everything for them. These glass ceilings have to be smashed by the person who is being contained by them, otherwise the freedom they gain won't be what it should be.

For most people, these barriers are a combination of ignorance ("I don't know if I can…" or "I don't know how…") and apathy ("I don't really care…") and these attitudes are generally held together by the glue of fear. This fear hits people in different ways – for some it's a fear of failure; they can't face the shame and disappointment of not "making it", and for others it's a fear of success; they simply can't face the weight of responsibility they think would be theirs to carry if they actually got to experience what they've been told could be their future reality.

So, breaking through these glass ceilings is essential if you want to see a person reach their potential in life.

Sometimes we want to just hit the limitation hard enough with all our truth and experience to smash it for them, so that the person you are working with can simply walk through to the next stage of life in freedom, but that would be a huge mistake. Giving them a breakthrough based on your life experience is not going to benefit them as much as you possibly think because they are probably conditioned to stay in the same place, and unless they learn how to overcome these things themselves they will be doomed to fall back into this pattern when things get hard again.

This conditioning is a little bit like putting a flea in a jar with a lid on and then taking it off after it's been there for a while. After the flea has been constantly bouncing its head off the lid of the jar it starts to limit its jumping so that it doesn't have any more negative experiences, and this is how limitations work in people's lives. Even if the lid of limitation in that person's life is removed by you, the chances are the conditioning remains. That's why removing the barrier for someone else doesn't actually remove the barrier, because only a reconditioning of how they personally perceive reality can actually make a difference. They need a new experience – a win – they need to overcome their limitations, and we need to lose the "hero" mindset of, "I'll do it for them…" The fact is that in these scenarios the person who is stuck needs a guide more than a hero, so that they are building their own strength and momentum as they push forward into the place of their ultimate destiny. I've found through bitter experience in my early days of working with broken people that we can sometimes cause more hurt to the person we're trying to help if we help them in the wrong way.

Have you ever heard the story of the boy and the caterpillar? I've added some details, but it goes something like this:

One day a boy saw a caterpillar making something and he asked what it was doing, to be told that it was forming a chrysalis (or cocoon) where it would stay until it had become transformed.

(This is a process called "metamorphosis". During this process the caterpillar actually digests itself, releasing enzymes to dissolve all of its tissues. In other words, it breaks down its old constituent parts to make way for something new to be formed. If you were to cut open a cocoon or chrysalis at just the right time, a literal caterpillar soup would ooze out. This process can seem messy to a casual observer. But it's not just falling apart in there, it has things called "imaginal discs", which have always been there and begin to take the shape of adult body parts even before the caterpillar forms a chrysalis or cocoon. Then, as it breaks down its old form these new parts take shape.)

Pretty amazing, huh?

Back to the story. At first the boy was excited, but after a while he became concerned. A butterfly was emerging, but it seemed to be struggling so hard to get out of the chrysalis that it looked like it couldn't break free by itself and was making no progress. So, the boy decided to help by making the hole bigger that the butterfly was already making for itself. This did indeed have the effect of speeding up the process and the butterfly soon came out. But as it emerged the boy could see that it had a swollen body and small, shrivelled wings. He continued to watch the butterfly, thinking that, at any moment, the wings would dry out and expand to support the swollen body. But that's not what happened. Instead, the butterfly just crawled around with a swollen body and shrivelled wings, unable to fly…

What the boy didn't understand was that the restricting cocoon and the struggle required for the butterfly to get through the tiny opening were nature's way of forcing fluid from the body of the butterfly into its wings so that it would be ready for flight once it achieved its freedom from the cocoon. It needed to struggle for itself in order to be prepared for its ultimate goal of flight.

Now, this is a nice story, but I believe it's one from which we can draw some parallels and learn some key lessons when trying to help someone to break free from a constricting situation or environment.

I personally have a biblical, supernatural worldview that informs me that there are no necessarily good or bad seasons that we go through in life – they are just different – and this viewpoint comes together positively when you realise that there are lessons to learn from each of these seasons you've been in. Learning the lessons of these times will then equip you to grow in ways that will help you later on in your life journey.

For example, I was addicted to heroin (and other drugs, but heroin was the big one). Was that ten-year season a good one for me? On the surface, of course not. It was dark and destructive, and I wanted out of it. Would I advise anyone to go down that route? Never! But did I learn anything and change anywhere? You better believe it! One crucial lesson, which I think we need to keep in the front of our thinking, was that what I was given at no cost to me while in that state held no value to me.

Let me explain what I mean by that with this example. I was given the opportunity in the late 1980s to be a guinea pig for the trial of a new form of detox at the Stapleford Clinic just outside London. A new pharmaceutical technique to accelerate the detox process had been developed and was called at that time "Nalorex" or "Naltrexone". I was taken to a clinic and prepped – heart rate, blood pressure etc. – and given a nappy (diaper) to wear and a gown – yes, a backless one – (which was pretty humiliating I can tell you!), and then I was given a cocktail of pills, including the Nalorex, to bring on the opiate withdrawal. The other pills in the cocktail I was given were supposed, in theory, to knock me out sufficiently until my body had undergone this accelerated withdrawal process. I won't go into the gory details, but it was horrible. However, it was really quick and after entering the clinic early in the morning I was able to be picked up to return home by the evening, having been informed that I was now opiate free! I was clean! It was what I'd wanted, but hadn't been able to achieve, for years. Then I was left with some Naltrexone pills to take every day to ensure I remained opiate free, as they supposedly blocked your brain's opium receptors so that even if you had a slip and took some heroin etc., the thinking was that it would have no effect, so you should just stop doing it. Unfortunately, it did nothing to help with your cravings. The problem with this is that all of a sudden, I was just a junkie without a habit. Nothing in my directional focus had changed. I still craved drugs as I was still, in my reality at least, blocked by this glass ceiling above me which held me for so long in this horrible way of life.

Looking back on this from my vantage point today I can see the real problem was that it was just too easy. What should have been a dream turned into a worst nightmare as I failed miserably at staying clean and fell back even harder into the madness of that whole lifestyle. If you didn't already know, addicts can be very resourceful, and I found that

I could switch the Naltrexone pills for something else so that while it looked as if I was taking them, I wasn't, and therefore their blocking effect stopped which enabled me to get high again.

For all his best intentions (and if I'm honest, I'm not completely sure of his agenda as he was later struck off), all the psychiatric doctor had done was to pick the fruit without dealing with the root, or in relation to our caterpillar story, had opened the cocoon for me without the necessary reconstruction work taking place. After that failure, I struggled on, getting worse and worse for another six or seven years until at age twenty-seven, having become a Christian in July 1995, I made the decision to enter the Victory Outreach Victory Home and take on its twelve-month programme. It was during this time that I began to own my freedom. There were some habits that I had to give up and others that I had to pick up. Throughout this process I was guided but not smothered or forced to do anything. I was given options and had to make decisions that had real consequences. I changed as I began the work of deconstruction and reconstruction of life. This eventually led to me directing Victory Homes, becoming an ordained minister and a regional church overseer, helping lead churches in different nations, all of which have involved massive responsibility, and I believe the only reason I could stand and serve in those roles was due to the very real training I received.

So, what can be practically learned from these illustrations? What I've learned to do when engaging with someone who is broken or hurting or addicted in some way, and is stuck beneath some kind of glass ceiling or barrier, is to ask myself four questions:

- Where can I help?
- How can I help?
- When should I help?
- What will help?

Let's look at these practically:

1) Where can I help?

 # You always start from where the other person is at - not from where you are at.

I think that it's incredibly important to be able to put yourself in someone else's shoes – to do your best to look at things from their perspective and not just your own. When you do that, it becomes clearer how and why they ended up where they were.

It might surprise you, but I think it's always best to start by identifying the root of the problem before trying to deal with the fruit of the problem. This might seem backwards but just getting someone to stop taking something or doing something is not necessarily the end of the matter, as we saw in my earlier example. Drugs or alcohol or other addictions, for example, are not necessarily the actual problem but are the result of the problem.

This doesn't have to mean going back to what happened

when they were a baby etc. (although I've known people abused at an early age or neglected and that has played a significant part in their later problems), but it helps to find out where everything started to go downhill. What does that ceiling look like to them?

For me, I think my problems with crime and addiction started with attachment issues, as my parents had me young and then went to work leaving me to be looked after by various aunts. Don't get me wrong, it was all healthy stuff, but it left something undeveloped in me. I then began to struggle with depression from about seven years old – I can remember clearly sitting in my parents' car outside a fish and chip shop on the Isle of Sheppey, en route to a weekend at my Nan's caravan at Leysdown, when a wave of "darkness" came over me along with the thought that there was no meaning to life. This "darkness" would invade my mind as I grew up, becoming progressively worse as puberty stormed my world. I now see that these two issues would manifest as I sought belonging in gangs and started self-medicating my "darkness", firstly with cannabis and then finally with cocaine and heroin.

So, one of the keys to digging out roots is by listening to that person's story so as to gain some clues. There are probably as many reasons for people's brokenness as there are people, so while there are certain pathways we want people to take, and certain finish lines we want them to cross, understanding where they're starting from can help prevent taking the wrong route and wasting time.

Therefore, the main key to answering the question of "Where can I help?" is getting to grips with the "cause" of the problem and what is keeping them in bondage, and if you can do that and help them see it, this will definitely have the long-term effect that's needed.

2) How can I help?

Provide a suitable environment and atmosphere for forward progress.

Never underestimate the power of "atmosphere" or environment.

In the book of Genesis, chapter one, we see God's template for his creation – first he created the heavens and the earth (environment), then he filled them. There was space before planets, earth before plants, seas before fish, sky before birds etc., and the right environment and atmosphere is crucial to helping someone break out of their negative situation into one where they can positively thrive, and this could be anything or anywhere that helps them to refocus on something or somewhere other than the situation they find themselves in.

For example, telling someone to stop taking drugs while they're still in the same environment where they take drugs is going to be difficult. Telling someone who's been long-term unemployed to just "find work" is unrealistic. People get stuck in patterns and rhythms and so helping them to break free means helping them to change the "space" they're in. For a drug addict, a residential community or rehab will help them to break their habit, because getting out of the old environment is often necessary before any real change can begin. For someone unemployed it's important they get into a workplace rhythm so voluntary work or an internship in a business or charity can help to recondition their lifestyle and prepare them for employment.

I've been in both these situations and have benefited from both of these environments. In my church we have both of these options available for people, and by simply creating these different atmospheres we've seen hundreds of men and women locally, and thousands worldwide, break free from limitations to become the people they were intended to be.

Going back to the "root" and "fruit" analogy, the key is to help them plant a brand-new tree – not just attempt to revamp an old one. This is where Christianity has been so incredible for me, as it's not just about "lifestyle change", it's about a "life exchange", where you give Jesus your wrongs and He gives you His rights. These rights include a clean slate from the past and new hope for the future. A new seed is sown, a new tree is grown, and new fruit is the result. Life becomes different and for many, this new life gets worked on and worked out until the old one is just a memory. At least, that's been my experience, which is why I want others to try it.

3) When should I help?

Make sure you're using the right timetable.

Not everyone moves at the same pace. There are reasons for this which can be as diverse as the people you're working with, but generally include a few common ones.

For some it's about counting the cost. They take time to really weigh up the options and the pros and cons of taking the step to change.

Then there are circumstances beyond your control. There are family complications or legal issues that might need a bit of untangling.

Above all there's the question of health. Are they physically able to make the moves they need to break through their limitations? On this note, though, it's wise to understand that the limitations, or glass ceilings, we're talking about here are ones mainly of the mind. They're "soul" issues – not just practical or physical issues. The reason I make this point is because I've seen disabled people completely free and fulfilled in their life, and I've seen able people completely bound by their perceived circumstances. Mental health is becoming one of the big issues of the twenty-first century so far, and this subject is as complex as the mind itself. If in doubt in this area, get specialist, qualified help wherever you can.

Really, though, there's no perfect time to help someone. The old adage that "If it's near enough it's good enough" is actually how you'll work. Get as many things in place as you can but there comes the time when you just have to risk it. Even brain surgeons work like this. There's always a risk. And sometimes you'll just have to do some emergency work to help someone. As long as you try, you have more chance of succeeding.

4) What will help?

Use the right tool for the right job.

When you've identified the root problem you then simply need to use the right tool. (More of this in another chapter).

For example, you don't use a chainsaw to take out a tooth, or a scalpel to cut down a tree. So sometimes, prescribed pharmaceutical drugs are not the answer – especially when dealing with addiction. They're okay for just maintaining the addict in a less chaotic form of addiction, but no good if you want to see them smash their limitations.

But in some other cases, pharmaceuticals work well, especially where there's a chemical imbalance of some kind. Applying the right tool for the right job will ensure the right outcome.

Often, conversation is powerful. Try some human interaction using your ears more than your mouth. Your ears are great tools!

Offering future options and possibilities is a great thing to do. People respond well to purpose and if you add real-time opportunities for some kind of physical involvement, you have a practical way of seeing people smash through their limits to achieve great things.

So, with all this in mind, don't worry if you've tried before and it didn't work out how you thought. I've found that most people don't hit the glass hard enough the first time due to their conditioning. Continue to encourage and empower them to smash that glass because when their breakthrough comes, it's one of the best things you'll ever see. Fulfilment awaits…!

THE FIXER OR FILLER?
(TWO QUESTIONS YOU
NEED TO ASK)

There are two main types of people you'll come across in your leadership journey. I call them "Fixers" and "Fillers".

These are not cheap stereotypes or labels, just convenient terms that have helped me to sort through all the various personality types and needs and desires of people that you will be called on to lead. It's important right here to qualify this by saying that everyone you meet is a unique individual and has different needs, but we're talking here about maximising your ability to provide a solution in a more effective way.

The first "type" of person (and I only categorise like this in order to prioritise my response to their need), will need leading from a place of brokenness to a place where the brokenness can be "fixed" (Once again, please be open to the terminology).

The second type of person is, for all intents and purposes, "fixed", with their broken areas mostly restored to wholeness, and will need leading into a place where they can begin to be "filled".

So, the uncomfortable question you need to ask is – "Is this person a 'fixer', or is this person a 'filler'?"

This may seem like a cut and dried notion, but it's very important if you don't want to be wasting your time trying to achieve something that is just not suitable – and let's be honest, your time as a leader is important, right? There's nothing more frustrating than investing your time, experience and expertise into someone who just seems to go and waste it. But that's exactly what will happen if you try to pour all your great "leadership equipping stuff" into a broken person. It's like pouring clean, fresh water into a bucket with a giant hole in it.

When I teach this principle in seminars, I like to use a visually memorable scenario. I take two 500ml bottles of water, a large clear bowl and a sharp knife. I ask the first question about the capacity of the bottle, which obviously is 500ml. I then ask a volunteer to pierce the bottle approximately a third of the way up from the bottom with the knife. The water contained in the bottle begins to pour out into the bowl. Then I pour the contents of the second bottle into the first and we all watch it pour straight out again. I then ask the next question:

"What is its capacity now?" People usually say, "500ml," and I then make this point: Its capacity now is at the level of its "wound" …

This wound can be some kind of moral failure, or the loss of a loved one, or a job. In fact, there are lots of different ways that something from outside can penetrate our lives causing pain and even leading to infection. Paraphrasing a saying, a wounded person can even "bleed over people who didn't cut them".

This is the reality of working with a "fixer". Your goal should firstly be to identify and help to bring healing or restoration to the "wound" – whatever that may be – as it will stop that person from retaining anything good or even positive that is poured or invested into them, and the reality is that this can happen to any one of us at any time.

The other "type" of person you'll come across is the "filler", who is like the bottle without a hole in it, and they are open and ready and hungry to be filled… but you keep trying to fix them and not fill them. There will be two frustrated people in the equation and a lot of valuable time wasted.

I don't like unnecessary, and especially limiting, labels, but some labels are helpful. An obvious example is tins of food – imagine not having labels on them? Think of the wasted time involved in opening them without knowing what they contain. You get the point.

Therefore, I think it's important to take a look at these two types of people in a bit more depth and how you recognise their different needs, so that you can lead them in the right way without the burden of frustration and wasted effort that comes from doing the wrong thing with the wrong type of person.

By my definition:

- **Fixers** – are people who are broken in some area of their life, be it mentally, emotionally or spiritually, and who don't have the capacity to receive or retain what you give them.

- **Fillers** – are people who are not broken in the same way (any more) and have the capacity to accept, and more importantly, process correctly and retain what you pour into them.

So, looking at these two types in more depth to begin with, we can recognise some of their identifying features, but before we look at them individually, it's important to remember a couple of things that mark the difference between people you can help and people you can't help, because the reality is that there are a few that are simply not ready to even be fixed unless some things change in their perspectives or attitudes. Until or unless these changes happen your best recourse as a leader is to make sure you have secure emotional boundaries in place whilst doing whatever you can to maintain them in a safe and stable condition. It's frustrating, but there are some common traits that I've encountered, and knowing them will keep you from spending valuable time that could be better used for someone else.

I know that for some people reading this it might sound too cut and dried, but please believe me when I say that working with broken, hurting people on the front lines of life can, at times, force you to use a form of spiritual triage. I've made many mistakes and ended up at times working with people who won't change, whilst there are others who desperately want and need the right input to propel them forward on the trajectory of transformation that miss out.

Here's some of the main characteristics of people who won't be helped:

Those who do not take responsibility for themselves

When there are continual excuses for mediocrity or failure and everyone else is blamed for whatever the problem is, it's impossible to make any forward progress. Someone who is unrepentantly irresponsible is going to be unfaithful, as faithfulness primarily has to do with owning and completing tasks. The irresponsible person will never finish what they are given to do – and it will be everyone else's fault why they didn't, including yours.

Those who are not transparent

There are also some people who create distance so they are not reachable or accountable, and only let others get so close before cutting them off. They do this because they fear allowing anyone, especially an authority figure, to see them for who they really are. Often, they are hiding or withholding something about themselves and that makes it impossible to treat the problem in the right way. It's a bit like going to see a doctor with a bleeding wound and leaving with pills for a bad back because of not disclosing the real need. It's almost impossible to help someone with that mindset.

Those who live in self-deception

Some broken people think they're doing fine, even when it's obvious to everyone else they're not. They learn to justify and normalise their situation and so stay the same. The big problem is that denial is the first step to deception, and this can, in fact, come up with some type of false reality that continually feeds their thoughts and feelings the things they want to hear about themselves and their key relationships. If you try to point this out to them, they become upset and blame you for either not understanding them or for wrongfully accusing them of something.

Those who insist on having a negative outlook on life

These people seem to always expect the worst in life, so they are never disappointed in anything or anyone, so whatever you do for them will never be enough. This is so draining. My wife and I worked with a woman once that never remembered any good thing that was done with her or for her. Whenever we wanted to speak to her it was always going to be something "negative". And I mean always! It was like that for ten years! That dark cloud can suck the joy out of everything it touches, so there comes a time when you realise that it's time to look at a different strategy.

One really important concept that gets overlooked or isn't understood is that good leadership doesn't work without good followership, and some people just don't follow very well. They can either try to stop the healing of their wound or even keep opening it back up, and there comes a point when you have to move on from that, because the reality is that there are just some people you can't help to grow because they won't do what needs to be done.

Before we move on, though, I've noticed that there is something that needs to be recognised in the makeup of those who want to help broken people – "sentimentality". Becoming sentimental with a broken person can even lead to co-dependent behaviour, and this is a trap. Leaders can't be sentimental, just as a doctor in an emergency department can't be sentimental either. Leading broken people needs the right heart, but it is also going to take the right mentality. That's why it's important to love people – but not to death! It's a sobering thing to realise that some broken people don't want to be fixed because being broken gets them the attention they crave.

So, with that in mind, let's look at our two types of people who can be helped – even though they're helped in different ways…

1) Fixers

Fixers are people with holes, or wounds. In other words, they need fixing, and where necessary, healing.

The difference with these people from those above is that even if they weren't aware of it at first, when you show them that they're "leaking", they respond in the right way.

Identifying this particular need is key. If you were to see a container that had a gaping hole in it, it's quite obvious that you wouldn't pour anything precious into it – it would pour straight out and be wasted. Some people who will cross your path will be like this. They will have a hole or wound that has become apparent to you and whilst it might seem hard to help these people at first, it's actually very simple. You just have to identify the hole and then fix it, and following are some common wounds that you'll probably come across:

- **Sin** – from a Christian perspective everyone starts off with this hole due to their disconnection with the creator God, and this hole can only be fixed by Jesus through faith and repentance as it is Jesus who offers forgiveness and reconciliation with God. For some people, that fixes them, and then they are off and running in terms of their capacity to be filled because repentance, necessarily, is an about turn – a change of mind or thinking or perception. Once that happens, a new direction is enabled, with new potential and possibility. There's still a journey to travel with all the ups and downs but the directional perspective is better.

- **Trauma** – this is big and can come from different events: an accident or bullying, domestic violence, or childhood neglect. How about war? We have a generation of battle-scarred servicemen and women dealing with the effects of the decades long "war on terror", who have wounds that often can't be easily seen, as well as those with life changing injuries. Any one of these things can wound a person and while some are long-lasting and often become buried, most can also happen at any time in life.

I've worked with people suffering from all of these at one time or another, from adults struggling with shame caused by childhood abuse to ex-soldiers suffering from PTSD (Post Traumatic Stress Disorder). Even my wife was wounded in this way when she was diagnosed with bone cancer (parosteal osteosarcoma) in her left leg in 2011. After what can reasonably be considered miraculous intervention (consultant's statement), she didn't have her leg amputated but instead is now the owner of the longest prosthetic implant of its kind in the world – a 24cm silver-coated titanium "bone", including knee and tibia, inside her own skin! The outcome was better than we hoped for, but the trauma wounded her and didn't heal for a few years.

- **Loss** – of a loved one especially, or possibly even a job or a role that the person enjoyed or had always desired. The loss of a loved one is one of those hard but simple things – hard due to its impact and the scope of the damage caused, but simple in that you know what needs to be focused on. This type of loss is markedly different from others and is by no means a quick fix. It takes time – lots of it – to get through, and often never gets fixed. Sometimes it just stops being all-consuming, but is always there in the background. The loss of a relationship or a job or role may be different in size and shape to that of a loved one, but once you identify one of these you can begin the process of reconstruction. It's never easy, but at least you know what's causing the breakdown.

- **Identity issues** – from low self-esteem on one hand to misplaced pride on the other, an unstable sense of who a person is can leave a gaping hole in their reality. Until it is healed, that person will struggle to retain anything that you give them in terms of information or responsibility because they keep getting lost in themselves. If you imagine a satnav/GPS in your car, before you can enter a destination or receive any directional instructions, you have to have your location locked into position. This is where a person's identity is so crucial, as it locks us in positionally in life. So, to fix this hole there needs to be a time of reorientation. Who are they? What are they supposed to be doing? These are a couple of the questions that need to be asked and answers offered to them to take hold of. When this happens, it's incredible how many other problems fade away.

- **Attachment issues and/or rejection** – not everyone forms strong attachments as infants and far too many people grow up in broken, dysfunctional families. Sometimes there's been sickness or depression that has created a relational distance and as people grow up, they struggle to form healthy bonds. Rejection is also a huge problem for many and can create a performance trap that they keep falling into, so building trust and healthy connections is a key component in helping someone with these very real issues break free from the destructive cycle that they may be trapped in. Some of this could take a long time as the wounds won't always close up quickly. But that's not always a bad thing if there is some deep-rooted poison that needs fully draining out. So, patience is necessary – I've even ministered to people for more than ten years as one of their wounds keeps reopening – but the desired end result is always healing, even though it's possible that in reality some extreme cases may not be fully healed this side of eternity.

- **Addiction** – maybe surprisingly, addiction is not, in my experience, a primary hole or wound. It's more like an infection that gets into a wound and spreads, causing destruction. Often when an addiction is overcome physically, there remains a real possibility that it will return if the wound or hole it entered through is still there. Using an analogy of a tree, the addiction is the fruit, but the wound is the root. To fully deal with the fruit and stop it growing you have to deal with the root. When the root problem is addressed the fruit of the addictive behaviour can dry up and grow no more. The temptation will always be there, but the need will be gone, which makes identifying root issues incredibly important when working with an addict. But this takes time and the building of a relationship based on trust and commitment, and sadly there are not many places an addict can go to where that happens. The lazy answer is to prescribe another drug to "maintain" and hopefully reduce the dose until the person is "clean", but far too many times that just leaves that person as a "junkie without a habit". It's just what I'd term "fruit picking". The problem is that "fruit season" will come back round again and if the original tree of addiction is still alive the result will be relapse, and the terrible cycle will begin again. Christian programmes, especially the residential ones, are ideally suited to dealing with this challenge as they are generally holistic, meaning that they look at the person as a whole and take time to address the real areas of need. In Victory Outreach International, since the beginning of the ministry in 1967, we've seen literally hundreds of thousands of lives transformed to various degrees, from the basic breaking of an addiction to the building of those lives into people fulfilling their potential in life. It's not easy, but if you'll take the time it's really worth it.

Getting fixed

Some of the phases of realisation that a wounded soul has to go through to be fixed are:

- I need to be fixed – "Acceptance"
- I want to be fixed – "Desire"
- I can be fixed – "Determination"
- I am being fixed – "Realisation"
- I have been fixed – "New Reality"

There is also a difference between a wound and a scar.

A wound is something that is still causing a problem. Maybe it's still fresh or causing pain or bleeding. Sometimes it was on the way to being healed, maybe even scabbed over, but then something caught it and opened it back up, or, more worryingly the wounded person either wouldn't leave it alone and kept picking at it, or it's become infected and seeps poison.

A wound

Wounds still need to be healed. And you will come across the "walking wounded" from time to time – those people who believe they can stagger forward regardless of the problems they have. Sometimes it's misplaced loyalty or bravery, but mostly it's simply a lack of self-care. At some stage they need to be "carefronted" – not just "confronted" – with the reality of their situation so that they can get their wound healed. (The main difference between these two being in the attitude it's being done with; carefronting being more of a concerned identification rather than just a pointing out of the problem). If this is not done these wounds will cause added problems over time until the wounded one will eventually collapse, and if that happens at the wrong time it could be disastrous for you and those associated with that person. There's nothing more tiring than dealing with unnecessarily "leaky" people.

A scar

A scar, on the other hand, was a wound at one time but has been healed. What remains is a mark or a memory that something tried to destroy that person – but failed!

It's commonly thought that successful people don't have any of these problems, but the truth is that most, if not all, successful people are covered in scars of one type or another because successful people are just those who refused to let their last failure be their last failure!

So, scars are healed wounds. They are also badges of honour! Be proud of your scars, because they are a living legacy of your victories over defeat, and make sure the people you work with recognise the difference.

Recognising a "fixed" person

As a leader looking for people to pour into, I always look for the evidence of scars. For the most part, they show that the person in question has overcome some heavy things and that gives them a certain substance which can be very useful to their further development.

In my experience, I think that you can recognise a fixed person by their "directional perspective" – are they constantly looking back *to* their problems, or are they looking forward *from* their problems? The direction of their focus will determine whether or not it's time to really start investing in them. After all, isn't it always easier to lead someone who's facing the right direction?

2) Fillers

Fillers are people who don't need to be fixed right now and are people with actual capacity. Because they have this real capacity, they can be filled and poured into.

All the wisdom and experience and knowledge that you've gained can be deposited in someone like this because they will be able to retain it and use it in the right way. I have always found it incredibly refreshing to work with someone that is open and hungry to learn because when you pour out what's inside you it makes room to be filled up again yourself. This principle can be seen in the apostle Paul's letter to his disciple Timothy, which is part of the New Testament:

> *And the things that you have heard from me among many witnesses, commit these to faithful men who will be able to teach others also.*

2 TIMOTHY 2:2 (NKJV)

In another version it translates like this:

> *You have heard me teach things that have been confirmed by many reliable witnesses. Now teach these truths to other trustworthy people who will be able to pass them on to others.*

2 TIMOTHY 2:2 (NLT)

Paul first reminds Timothy that the stuff he's sharing actually works and has been reliably confirmed. This is important, I think, as it provides a sense of reality to what's being shared. The quoting of other people is great in an academic setting but what is more powerful is when you can actually apply what you're teaching to instances in your own life. After all, it's easier to follow footsteps than signposts.

Another thing that is key to this process is to understand that *you're number two in a four-part process of forward growth.* We should all be following somebody and then we should all be training somebody else who can then do the same. If this ideal was to be fully realised, we would see amazing transformation take place in our societies.

Then Paul sets out his standards of the people he's looking for to pour into. There are two criteria: they need to be faithful and able. This is a really important combination if you don't want to waste your time by pouring the wrong thing into the wrong person.

Here's an equation I use that's helped me:

$$\text{Faithfulness} - \text{Ability} = \text{Fantasy}$$
$$\text{Ability} - \text{Faithfulness} = \text{Frustration}$$
$$\text{Faithfulness} + \text{Ability} = \text{Fruitfulness}$$

The first scenario is where there's someone who always turns up for football practice but just can't play football. They're faithful but just not able. Or how about the one who turns up regularly and on time for every choir practice, but when they open their mouth to sing, they sound like a wolf? It's all a fantasy. By all means find some way to reward their faithfulness – just don't make the mistake of empowering their fantasy, otherwise someone will end up hurt.

The second scenario is when you know the person in question can do what needs to be done – sometimes even better than you – but they either don't turn up or are constantly late. Isn't that so frustrating? They have all the talent in the world but they either take it for granted or are just lazy. My dad used to tell me that, "hard work will always overtake talent that doesn't work hard," and I've seen people who, while not brilliant at what they do, become very competent at what they do simply due to their work ethic. And I've also, sadly, seen brilliant people end up nowhere because they just weren't faithful with their gift.

The last scenario is the ideal. People that turn up at the right time, on time, who have the ability, both natural and acquired, and just receive and retain everything you give them. And then when they, in turn, release it in their turn to other faithful men who then do the same – the impact you can make is quite literally quadrupled. Now that's what I call being fruitful and effective!

The most amazing thing I've discovered, though, is that people who have needed fixing often become the most effective future leaders. They're not striding off strongly in the wrong direction or even limping in the right direction. They are under no illusions as to what life is all about and they have faced the worst that can happen and have survived, so now they are grateful. And gratitude will affect your attitude which will in turn affect your altitude.

These are the ones who will do great things in a great way. There might not seem like there's many of these quality people, but I think that if more leaders were able to identify these things it would open the floodgates of potential and possibility that are available in the lives of the people who cross our paths.

Therefore, try to identify the type of person you have in front of you as quickly as possible. Then you can tailor your efforts so that everyone you work with has the possibility to become everything they were created to be.

So why not start immediately with those people in front of you? Because in a year from now you'll have wished you'd started today…

THE TOOLS
OF YOUR TRADE

Working with broken people is like going to war and crafting a masterpiece at the same time.

For this task you'll need the right weapons and tools. There are going to be battles you fight against opposing forces and personal mindsets, so you need to be prepared. My view is that if you are intent on doing this work then you are first of all a warrior, and then you become a craftsman as you actually do the work of leading broken people.

There's a wonderful book in the Old Testament called Nehemiah where God's people are rebuilding the broken walls of Jerusalem. There comes a point in chapter four where this necessity of fighting and building at the same time becomes crystal clear, and whether it's rebuilding walls or people, the reality will be the same.

With this in mind it's necessary to become familiar with your tools and how to use them. The reason it's important is that any time you're asking people to change, there will be situations that will oppose you and genuine concerns that those people will have. This is the battle ground and when you understand what tools to use, you'll have more chance of coming through it with another transformed person with you. When you take the time to meet the personal concerns that people naturally have, and you have the necessary tools to work with, you'll win a lot of trust and be able to generate and maintain the momentum necessary for the change to be a successful one.

I've found there are six predictable questions that people have when they are asked to change. Sometimes the sequence changes, but the conscious and unconscious things that run through people's minds when changes are on the menu remain the same:

The first question is usually:

1) What is the change that's needed?

This has to do with information. Your tool here is truth.

Truth is powerful. Truth sets people free. So be honest about their condition. Try to get them to see what their life really looks like, not just what they've fallen into believing it looks like. Most broken people get caught in the trap of trying to justify why they are the way they are, and will usually try to blame everything or anyone else for their condition. The first obstacle to face and overcome is denial, because that mindset is a massive barrier to break through. Denial is not just a long Egyptian river; it's a real problem and the clearer information you can provide to someone about the need to change, the better.

Just don't forget to speak the truth in a loving way. Someone once said that giving truth without love is like kissing someone with bad breath. What should be something good can be spoiled by not paying attention to something important.

A question that always runs through a person's mind after this is:

2) How will the change impact me personally? What will I gain?

This next question is of a personal nature. Your tool here is your personal story (testimony), or even the stories of other people that might be relevant.

Give examples of success. I remember my dad telling me that, "Once seen is ten times told," and it's true. If you can show what you mean or point someone in the direction of someone else who has positively negotiated change in some area then you're halfway there, and if you can align them with someone who is walking out the same sort of change you've advocated, then better still. I always say that, "footprints are better than signposts," where the process of change is concerned. In other words, there's no substitute for real experience where change is concerned. You can learn and teach some great stuff academically, but nothing beats practical application and experience for authenticity, and it's that realism that captures people's imagination. If you can get them to visualise the possibility, then you have a strong chance of them taking steps to make what they have imagined a reality.

But please note that *delegation* of responsibility is different than *abdication* of responsibility at this point in the journey. The temptation can creep in to abandon that person and let someone else take up the slack, but the only time you fully release your engagement is when the person you're working with is stable enough to walk on their own two feet. At the very least, keep following up on them. One church near us had a situation with a man struggling with addiction who was married to a woman in their congregation. They didn't know what to do and after trying their best for some time to help him they eventually contacted us at Victory Outreach, due to the fact I knew the pastor quite well. The man in question was from Salford, in Greater Manchester, where our respective churches are situated, and after considering what would be best, I found him a place in one of our Victory Homes in Liverpool where his life began to completely turn around. While this process was ongoing, though, my pastor friend who had originally brought him to us still kept in contact with him. The church prayed for him and sent encouragement to him constantly. This was a massive help during his changing process as he felt like he hadn't just been completely dumped out of his old life. His life would never be the same but at least there was some continuity to the change, and a major key to his change was the fact that he was surrounded by changed and changing people from the same sort of background he'd come from. Every story was similar, and the footprints were right there. Success is contagious, so if you can get someone to see it or be around it you can be sure they will catch something of it for themselves.

When a person begins to see the need for and the possibility of a positive change, they'll want to know how to go about it.

3) What do I do first? What do I do next?

This addresses the need for implementation.
Your tool here is structure.

It's very important that people know step by step what is going to be expected of them during their process. This provides security and hope. People that are kept in the dark or stay ignorant of these steps can either freeze and get stuck or become afraid and run. Putting a structure in place – and it can be a loose one to begin with – enables positive progress to continue. It could be as simple as a daily timetable of achievable goals to begin with, adding some progress goals for a month at a time. You'll be surprised how helpful these things are to someone who has been used to living in chaos. Wherever things have broken down in someone's life and they're confused and off balance, knowing clearly the next thing to do is like being able to grab hold of a rope in a pitch-black cave which becomes their lifeline to freedom. Don't complicate things and remember that simple structures are the best.

The next thing that is commonly asked has to do with the reality of the change:

4) Where am I changing? Is all the effort worth it? Is the change making a real difference?

The question here is regarding the impact the changing process is having. Your tool in this instance is evaluation.

Regularly *inspect what you expect*. Have consistent check-ups with them and point out to them how far (or not!) they have come. Encouragement can work wonders, even if they haven't fully met your expectations. If they have moved forward an inch, instead of the mile you were hoping for, that's okay.

Celebrate the win with them. Then challenge them with the next expectation. I call this the "praise sandwich". Start with your first slice of bread – or encouragement or praise for what they've achieved – then add the "meat" of what they still need to do. Then "sandwich it up" with another piece of encouragement to build their sense of possibility going forward. When you do this consistently, you'll find that momentum is maintained because the fact is, *you're only aware of the growth you measure*. This becomes a powerful barometer to gauge the next step, because whenever someone sees growth it releases the desire to press on to the next challenge.

By now you've probably realised that helping people is best done with others because it's true that "teamwork makes the dream work". So, the question becomes:

5) Who else should be involved?

This involves the need for cooperation.
Your tool here is your network of contacts.

I'm convinced that relationships are the basis of every healthy thing and rather than networking for the sake of it you should do your best to build relational connections with people for mutual benefit. My friend, Matt Bird, currently CEO of Cinnamon Network International, has captured this concept brilliantly in his book, *Relationology*. When you have this relational base, comprising of people who know you and who can usually do what you can't, you have a pool of healthy resources to help you help others.

Different people have different needs and you may not have all the experience or knowledge needed. But someone has, so the key is to bring in key people to help at key times. We already saw this can work with people's personal stories of change, but now you can add real expertise to the mix. From professional counsellors to careers advisors, lawyers and medical professionals, the list goes on. If you're not doing that, I'd encourage you to start. I know it can seem difficult if you're not used to doing it, but it's possible. I'm a bit of an introvert by nature and find social settings awkward to negotiate, but when I have the opportunity to talk about my passion for helping people it opens up conversations with other people that are like-minded and evens out the playing field. I've met people from nearly every walk of life and profession, and some of those relationships have been massively helpful in enabling people to move forward in life from a place of brokenness to the possibility of fulfilment.

Then lastly, but definitely not to be overlooked, there's the question of maintenance:

6) How can we keep the change going?

This is about follow-up.
Your tool here is accountability structures.

Accountability is a much-overlooked tool. I think it's because it can be misused and become controlling when misunderstood, both by those utilising it and those who are being asked to be accountable. But when it works correctly it provides a canopy or covering which can protect the one who commits to it. In a nutshell, accountability has to do with being responsible and willing to answer for your actions and has to do with how someone conducts themselves.

I don't just preach this; I live it and actually make myself accountable to several people in different ways. Firstly, I'm mutually accountable to my wife, Vicky. We share details of our lives with each other and keep no secrets (except when I'm getting her a gift, of course), including our whereabouts, finances, people we meet and online habits. On top of that I have an overall covering as part of the Victory Outreach International Ministry. As a licensed/ordained minister I hold my credentials with them, which brings with it certain expectations and benefits. I'm also in an accountability group in Manchester, where I live and work. I have certain friends, who are also ministers, who I give permission to hold me to account with my life and work. This is also mutual, and the benefits are that I know I'm protected from myself and from giving in to one of the many temptations the world we live in presents, and if I start becoming wacky, I have people I trust who will pull me up.

Having these accountability structures can go a long way to enabling the positive changes that people make to keep progressing forward in the right direction.

A couple of other ways to build in these structures on top of the purely relational ones are conferences, where mutual accountability can be had on a larger scale, and involvement in work or ministry. If you can get to the point where a fixed person you've worked with gets involved in some way reaching other broken people, you've cracked it. It's amazing how serving others who face similar challenges to the ones you've overcome yourself can really push you onwards towards a sustained future filled with the type of freedom you've always longed for.

Learning to serve shifts people's focus from themselves and allows them to truly fly free. This is Jesus's pattern and it works.

So, know your tools and keep them sharp and ready for use. The writer of Ecclesiastes puts it like this:

If the iron is blunt, and one does not sharpen the edge, he must use more strength, but wisdom helps one to succeed.

ECCLESIASTES 10:10 (ESV)

Having the knowledge of what to do, and then doing it in the right way at the right time, is wisdom, and if you want to succeed in helping people to change you need it in huge amounts. Use your tools wisely, then, and watch as someone amazing emerges from the darkness of their old existence, and you'll have the satisfaction of having played your part in seeing that treasure come out of darkness.

THE "SATNAV"/ "GPS" PRINCIPLE (MOVING FORWARD IN THE RIGHT DIRECTION)

Making progress is only good if you're heading in the right direction.

When I was an addict, I started somewhere by smoking cannabis and drinking, and then I made progress into becoming a fully-fledged junkie, and obviously that type of progress was unhealthy. You'll be surprised by how many people put time and talent and treasure into heading in the wrong direction. Some things, like addiction, are obvious examples of this problem, but there are more subtle areas that people make progress in, that when examined objectively, are taking people away from their place of purpose and potential towards a place of ineffectiveness. The truth is that you can even be doing the right thing but going in the wrong direction. You can work hard at the wrong thing. Or you can plant (or sow) good stuff in the wrong places, and the result of going in the wrong direction is frustration. I think one of the most frustrating things is either losing something or getting lost. I've got lost many times in my life and I can pinpoint two main reasons why – either I was ignorant of the direction I needed to go in and I was just too proud to ask for directions, or I didn't follow the directions I was given. And I also found it true that while ignorance and rebellion play their part, one of the biggest, yet most subtle, of the enemies of direction is distraction. If your focus can be captured by something else, you can move away from the direction you should be going in.

Therefore, making sure you are focused on going in the right direction is an essential part of reaching your potential, and when you're working with people, especially broken people, this is one of the major differences between success and failure.

So, how can this whole directional focus process be simplified? It clicked for me the first time I used a mobile satellite navigation device (satnav/GPS) to go on a journey. It became so easy – there were no unwieldy maps or complex sets of directions – it just became an exercise in following instructions and the concept of how a satellite navigation system (GPS) works is very simple:

- First it locks in your location… which speaks of position.
- Then you enter your destination… which speaks of purpose.
- Finally, it gives you directions… which speaks of process.

As a bit of background, the development of the global positioning system, known either as GPS or "satnav" in the UK, revolutionised the way we would travel from one place to another.

I actually met an American gentleman on a trip to Mexico called Joe Dwyer, who really confirmed this whole idea to me. We began a casual conversation between sun loungers as our wives lay relaxing, and after some time he told me that one of his "claims to fame" was the fact that, as a major in the United States Air Force, in the summer of 1980, he commanded the first ever journey that used GPS as a navigation system, called "Project Speckled Trout", from Andrews air force base to Hickman in Honolulu.

GPS had originally been developed for another, more destructive, use, but the US military was exploring the possibility of using it as a new system to simplify travel.

Previous to this, the air force had flown using the "NATRAK" system, which was much more involved and complex and reliant upon calculations.

This system has helped me a great deal in understanding the idea of directional forward progress, which is really important when leading and signposting people from a place of brokenness to the fulfilment of their potential. Discovering and developing these three areas has enabled many people to get on track and to stay on track, so let's dive into these things and see what unfolds:

1) Locking in your location

This speaks about your identity – who are you? Who do you belong to? Where are you and where do you fit?

This is so important because understanding your identity is the antidote to insecurity and whoever discovers this unlocks a door that ultimately leads to fulfilled destiny. I believe this is true for all of us and it's really important for those of us that work with people in this area to have this understanding set and solid in our own lives, because you can't lead people where you've never been – because when you try to do that it makes you more like a travel agent than a leader, as it doesn't matter how incredible your gifting and experience is if you're not credible to the people you're leading. Always start by looking at yourself and evaluating where you're really at before attempting to tell someone else where they're at. That way, you'll both end up in the right place.

The challenge is, who will you believe and what voice will you listen to and end up trusting in? It's important to understand that there are many voices in life with different motives that clamour for your attention, and far too often, people who struggle to find and stay on a straight course are the ones who listen to the loudest, most insistent voices. But I am of the conviction that the quiet, consistent voice – not the loud, insistent voice – is the one we need to hear and respond to with faith and in trust, and as a follower of Jesus I believe that the voice that needs to be listened to, that quiet, consistent voice which has our best future in mind, is the voice of the creator God. After all, the creator knows why He put you on earth, He knows where He placed you and where He wants you to get to in life, and He knows what you need to do or stop doing so that you can become everything He has made you for.

For this identity location to become a solid reality, you need to ask honest questions of yourself, accept the reality of your position, and then have regular evaluation to make sure you're not trying to set off from a place you're not actually at – because if you try to move from a place of fantasy or denial, it doesn't matter what direction you go in, you won't reach your desired destination.

As a Christian, it was important for me to get to grips with this early in my journey. Studying the Bible was essential in this realisation, and I found the letter to the Hebrews in the New Testament especially helpful in this. It was clear that I didn't earn my position through my own efforts as a Christian, just as I didn't earn my place in my natural family. My spiritual life, like my natural life, was a gift that I simply had to receive.

Looking at chapter 10 we can read about this concept.

Under the old covenant, the priest stands and ministers before the altar day after day, offering the same sacrifices again and again, which can never take away sins.

HEBREWS 10:11–18 (NLT)

(All religious systems are like that – you constantly have to do something or sacrifice something to please your god, but the good news gospel version of Christianity is different in this respect.)

> *But our High Priest (Jesus Christ) offered himself to God as a single sacrifice for sins, good for all time. Then he sat down in the place of honour at God's right hand.*

V12

(Look at the contrast – the standing of the priests indicates unfinished work that is never done [there were no chairs in the sanctuary]. The sitting of Jesus indicates that His work of sacrifice is finished, and that He has been exalted to the place of supreme honour…)

If we borrow an example from real estate and the idea of an interest-only mortgage, we can get a sense of how this worked…

With a mortgage of this type, only the interest on the capital amount is paid, leaving the capital amount untouched. While this sum is still owed the interest must continually be paid. The person paying this can live in the house – technically as an "owner", but in reality, just an "occupier" – and still has the capital amount hanging over their head, so the ownership is really an illusion. If the house was sold, you'd only profit a little if the value increased but the lender would receive the lion's share.

I came to understand that this is like dead religion with its sacrifices and ways of earning approval from its god – with lots of effort expended but no great reward for it or any real freedom to move forward.

But then Christ comes and qualifies to be able to pay off that capital sum in full, meaning the interest payments are no longer needed.

There he waits until his enemies are humbled and made a footstool under his feet.

V13

This speaks ultimately about justice in that, although we don't understand everything that happens to us in this life, eventually God will make it all right and our eternal enemies will be dealt with – which is a very satisfying thought…

For by that one offering he forever made perfect those who are being made holy.

V14

This is it and is something so powerful it needs to be broken down a bit.

There are two important terms here – "perfect" and "holy" – which we can briefly look at.

The word "perfect" is key to our identity and location and can be very misunderstood. In the original Greek text, it is "teleios", which has the definition of:

Perfect, (a) complete in all its parts, (b) full grown, of full age, (c) specially of the completeness of Christian character.

But most importantly, it declares that the mission of Christ, which began at his virgin birth and was completed through his death on the cross and subsequent physical resurrection from the dead, brought to completion (or perfection) the plan of God to re-establish a full and intimate relationship with humanity.

There is something incredibly powerful about this – you are perfect in Christ…! That's where you are at.

This idea of perfection and holiness – which together speak of a goal reached in maturity or completeness – and holiness which means set apart or different – shows us two concepts – position and direction – which are incredibly important in our journey towards our ultimate destination.

First there is the matter of "position", which is what locks in where you are, and the amazing truth of the position of believers before God is that they are *perfect*, or maybe it makes things clearer by using the word "complete". God has forgiven all of their sins through Christ's sacrifice, and He has imputed Christ's perfect righteousness to them, and this is the basis of our standing before God.

In Greek, the perfect tense in Hebrews 10:14 speaks of the permanence of this perfection by describing past tense salvation (justification). So, (active) believers are forever positionally "perfect" in Christ.

As a follower of Christ, that's where you are. If life was set out like a map with a pointer that says, "Here you are," it would be pointing to God's perfect presence.

Then, secondly, the "direction" speaks about the practice of believers with this Christ-focused direction, pointing to the fact that believers are being sanctified or made holy which is an ongoing process.

This practice of a life of sanctification – being made holy – is worked out as you grow in obedience, sometimes with the need for God's discipline, and in essence means that the practice of believers is that they are being sanctified or made holy and are continually growing in holiness in thought, word, and action.

This word, holy – in Greek, "hágios" – has the idea of a different ("unlike"), other ("otherness"), holy for the believer, and can mean "likeness of nature with the Lord", because of being "different from the world and its autonomous system".

This position is granted instantly at the moment of saving faith – with the practice being worked out over a lifetime of growth in obedience – but this Biblical notion of "holy" and "sanctified" does not begin with your character – it begins with relationship, or your "belonging to God".

Can you see how knowing this is so crucial when leading people into their potential destiny? The essential fact is that when your location is locked in and your identity is solid, you can then begin to set your preferred destination.

2) Entering your destination

You have to know where you want to go.

This may seem obvious, but it's harder than you think it is, generally because we rarely ever clearly see the fulfilment of our individual destiny in our mind's eye. As a Christian, you have a hope that one day you'll be received into eternity by God and have a resurrected body so that you will no longer be subject to sickness or decay or death, and that's probably the best destination you can enter because that's as far as we are promised we can go.

Also, this phase becomes challenging because it involves a process and it takes time. If we're honest, we want things to happen now. Waiting and working out the steps and stages and challenges of our process is hard. But so is being stuck or staying in the same condition or position. So, we have to choose our hard.

Some people struggle in this area, though, as they either don't have that hope or they're setting their sights on the wrong thing. I've known people set their sights on places that are going to be impossible for them to reach, just as if you set an address on a satnav/GPS in a place that is in a restricted area, or an area where there are no roads, such as the top of Mount Everest. Some places we set our sights on are just not reality. But how about those people who are envied, for their wealth or prominence in society? Can't we become like them? The answer is that of course it's possible, but you'll generally find it rare that they actually set out to be rich or famous. Most, if not all of them, simply followed their passion – that was the destination they set, and they then just followed the instructions to get where they eventually got to.

So, when entering your destination, the most important questions to ask are, "What's my passion? What brings me alive just thinking about doing it?"

After all, life is to be enjoyed – not just endured, right? We should never underestimate the power of passion in setting a direction.

But what about your destination being a person to become…? Then the focus shifts a little…

We can fall into the trap of limiting ourselves by almost demanding that we should be this or that (a pastor, or prophet, or evangelist, or top business person, or sports star, or a celebrity, or whatever…), and so we don't embrace the journey and process to being who God wants us to be…

I once heard this:

"Young riders pick a destination and go… old riders pick a direction and go…"

That direction idea means simply following Jesus for the rest of our life. Our ultimate destination in Christ on earth is that we should be His representatives – or "imagers" – here on earth, growing in holiness as we journey with God.

So, God created human beings in his own image.
In the image of God, he created them;
male and female he created them.
Then God blessed them and said, "Be fruitful and
multiply. Fill the earth and govern it…

GENESIS 1:27–28(A) (NLT)

This role is incredibly important as it's the desired destiny of God's people. We become this through the process of what I think of as "emergence", like a pot from clay or a statue from a block of marble.

God shapes us from the raw material and He uses time and circumstances to do it.

In fact, it happens as we simply follow His instructions…

3) Following the instructions

Moving on with the satnav/GPS analogy, once your location is locked in and your destination is set, the next thing that happens is you're given instructions. These instructions are step by step and this is a crucial truth to understand when trying to move forward in life. I've known many people that want their whole future laid out for them, but don't take notice of or follow through on the first step. What would happen if your device told you to, "Turn right in one hundred metres," and you travelled for fifty metres and stopped? The answer is – nothing! You could sit there for a month and not get another instruction. The key to learn is that you only get a new instruction when you've completed the last one.

That's why mentors and coaches and leaders are important as they have viewpoints which are more objective and can help with the next step of the instructions that enables future progress to be made.

If you're one of those "voices", here's a little, but really important, note for you – you're only responsible for the advice or instructions you give. You're not responsible for what people do with it. Just as a satnav/GPS device can't be blamed if someone ignores it, neither should you beat yourself up if someone ignores you.

These principles work if you work them. Once someone has been honest with who they are and where they're really at in life – and they've set their desired destination – and kept following the advice and making the necessary moves – they have every chance of reaching the places in life they were created to experience.

So, let the journey begin…

THE "DIAMOND" PATHWAY (THE PROCESS OF TRANSFORMATION)

People are more valuable than any treasure you can think of.

I'm here writing this because someone found me and dug me out of the dark place I was stuck in. I'm an ex… (add drugs and crime and other nasty stuff to that), but I've changed. Now I'm one of God's men, and I'm fortunate that I've been trained by other men who knew what it took to mine for treasure. Follow me here – look what a miner does. He goes into dark places looking for raw materials that have the potential to become objects of value. That's what Jesus did, and that's what we have to do today.

You see, while people are tripping on the "decline of men in the church", men are being reached in the unlikeliest of places. The problem is that too many observers have a consumer mindset. They're looking for the finished product – shiny and well-set and packaged just right. And they overlook the bits of rough, dirty rock that are pulled out of the inside of the earth. But it is precisely these rough diamonds that will bring value to the church. First, however, they must be cut and polished. This is the trick, and this is where things get uncomfortable. But don't worry. The thing is, men like getting trained. But only if there is something worth training for. Men love adventure. They love the sense of achievement that comes from applying themselves to something and stretching and growing, and the feeling that comes from overcoming and being victorious. Men love getting smacked between the eyes by the truth of the word of God. They love reality. They want to stand for something and reach for something that is worthy and noble and worth their time. I believe the Christ life is the best life and my fulfilment comes when I find that earth-covered bit of treasure and start the training process. Sure, it's a challenge. But that's what catches men. And it's so worth it.

What about women, you ask? Can the same idea be applied to them? My answer is that of course it can, and quite often there are more of them being found than men. My wife does this better than me, though, because of her innate understanding of her gender. It's really about context, and even though they love adventure and challenge and truth as well, women mostly respond to different stimuli than men. There are subtle differences in style, but I've found that the principle is the same, as is the process. After all, a diamond is a diamond.

This process in a person's journey of transformation, whatever their sex, has several general stages that they will go through. It's also important to understand that each stage, while being sequential, can take different lengths of time to work through.

There are many different people that have a part to play during the different stages of this journey, but it's incredibly fulfilling being involved in something from start to finish. Very few people have that opportunity and it's actually quite rare when leading people to have found the people you later train. Mostly we find ourselves joining in at some point of the process to add our skills or experience to the mix, a little bit like being part of a production line at a factory. There's absolutely nothing wrong with that and as long as we add value to the ongoing process and do not hinder it with our input in any way, that input is worthwhile and probably even necessary. But like assembling a puzzle it's always handy to know what the actual picture on the box looks like. And I discovered a way of looking at the picture of the process of growth in a person's life from brokenness to fulfilment that has become absolutely invaluable.

I call this the "Diamond Method". It all fell into place when I happened to watch a documentary about the De Beers Diamond company. I became fascinated as the commentator described the process that a diamond went through on its journey to becoming one of the most valuable items on the planet. It struck me that people are actually the most valuable things on the planet and too many are buried under a mass of stuff that is keeping their potential and value hidden.

According to their website (debeersgroup.com), the De Beers Group of companies, originally formed in 1888, are "involved in almost every stage of the diamond pipeline: exploration, mining, sorting, valuing and selling rough diamonds; marketing and selling polished diamonds and jewellery; and developing synthetic diamonds for industrial use."

As the programme detailed these different stages, I began to see how similar this was to the process of development from a sense of worthlessness and obscurity that a person who has endured some measure of brokenness has come from, to a place of enjoying the brilliant and multifaceted life of dignity, belonging and destiny held in their future.

This process looks like the discovery of a diamond and its journey through the different stages of becoming the thing of beauty and value that we associate with them – and the diamond process is compatible with humans and what Christians call "discipleship".

It's interesting to note that according to Jewish rabbis, scripture has seventy faces, or facets, like that of a diamond. When light enters a diamond, it is reflected and refracted throughout its carbon atom matrix, revealing an array of dazzling colours. However, if the diamond is not cut properly, the refraction of light is greatly diminished.

The word of God is the greatest tool used in forming a soul, and when it's used correctly it will enable that soul to be one that reveals the beauty and value that its creator intended for it, so it's important to understand the process.

This process is really helpful if you're thinking of starting a church or ministry or a charitable organisation and you don't have massive outside input in terms of manpower. Sometimes it's just you and your spouse or a couple of like-minded people with a vision. That was my experience as my wife and I made our way from London to Manchester to take on the role of building a Victory Outreach church, pretty much from scratch. Even though we're part of an international movement of churches, we've never had much in the way of support, either financially or in terms of human expertise, so we had to learn quickly on the job. It forced us to mine for and train the people who would eventually help us to get things moving. Many are still with us and are growing beyond their wildest dreams, and we also now see "experts" in different areas joining us on our journey, because growth and success are attractive. But at the beginning of anything you've got to be prepared to work hard and get your hands dirty if you're going to build something that will make a difference to people's lives.

Let's define the journey:

Stage 1: Searching for source material

It should come as no surprise that this part is not played by everyone – at least not intentionally – although it can be said that Christians and those who work with broken people should always be open to and ready for it. But it's not easy. When a mining company looks for a place to mine, they utilise different methods. Without stretching things too far I believe that these methods can be transferred from the diamond realm into the searching out of broken people. After all, many are crying out for help but, like a potential piece of diamond hidden in a mountain, they can't free themselves.

Obviously, there are geological and statistical factors involved but one of the most common methods of search is when news comes from a local person that a certain area has been known to have diamonds. In my experience, word of mouth is one of the most effective ways of finding out where someone is struggling. Then a team will be sent to investigate and search for them. With diamonds you can often find them quite close to the surface as they would've been pushed outward by magma, molten rock, from some type of disturbance. Many of the biggest diamond mines in the world began like this, and another important thing to consider when embarking on this type of search is it's usually better to respond to a hurt that's been exposed than to go digging into something to try to expose it. That can be devastating to the person's environment and can even lead to more pain.

Quite often, myself and like-minded and committed people have gone to places on intervention teams to try to find some "diamonds". Areas where drugs or prostitution are known to be a big problem can sometimes bring us face to face with exposed problems and people who desperately want to change but who either don't know how or don't have the motivation within themselves to even try. I can recount more stories than we have space for in these pages of some of these amazing people, but here's a short one to illustrate why it's important to search:

Brian's story

"Waking up on a hospital bed, my eyes were hurting, my body was hurting, I realised that I was still alive! It hadn't worked! I had taken a load of tablets hoping to end my sorry life. At only twenty years of age I was done! I was addicted to heroin, tablets and weed. My family were finished with me. My brother was trying to kill me. No one wanted to know me. I was eating out of bins.

"All of my young life, I remember being in and out of women's aid shelters and always ending up back with my mum's partner. Their relationship was volatile with alcohol, and he was not my dad, so I felt excluded. I felt rejected all of my life; I always felt worthless and unwanted.

"I remember not long after my futile attempt at taking my life, I was invited to hear an 'addict team' from Victory Outreach London speak at the People's Church in my hometown of Falkirk in Scotland. After hearing their stories of transformation from addiction I spoke to Pastor Paul Lloyd and agreed to enter into the Victory Outreach Men's 'Victory Home' in March 2001. It wasn't easy, but I graduated in May 2002. I moved in to a place with some guys who had also graduated from the programme and then in 2004 I got married to my wife, Fiona. Since then I've been in full-time employment and, moving to Manchester, I linked up again with Pastor Paul, and in 2013 my wife and I became the directors of the Victory Outreach Manchester women's home. We struggled to have children but decided to adopt in 2017 and needed to leave our position due to the adoption agency rules. But now we are the proud parents of our beautiful little daughter, Georgie. I have also faced and beaten cancer in that time.

"It's been a tough journey, but I can say that I'm a changed man – free from every addiction and living life in a way that was once beyond my dreams, and I'm grateful for everyone who has helped me along the way. That's why I love doing the same, now, for others who were like me."

Stage 2: Identifying potential

But then when you've discovered a "diamond", you have to identify whether it really is what it seems or whether it's something else instead. This is really key if you want to be able to do right by it. When the "diamond" is a person you will then be able to either signpost them to the organisation or service that will benefit them most, or perhaps even begin to walk with them through the next stages of their process. For example, not everyone needs to go into some sort of intensive programme, although some most definitely do. Some people need specialist mental or medical care. Others will respond to focused time spent with them in a mentoring relationship, whilst a few just need a hand-up and a push in the right direction. Then there are those frustrating times when you realise it's not a diamond after all. It's not that people can't change – it's just a fact that some people won't change. What's important is that you do everything you can to get the assessment right as early as you can.

Let's look back to our valuable rocks again. When determining whether something is a diamond to be worked with or not, there are some things to consider:

1. Firstly, they come in all shapes and sizes and they don't necessarily look like the stereotype. When you find a diamond in its rough state it doesn't look as

impressive as it one day will. I've known addicts who function in a professional environment as well as someone who is dirty because they're homeless. I've also known people with a background of abuse who are excellent parents or spouses. You often have to look deeper than the surface.

2. Secondly, it's more than likely that a little surface rubbing will reveal what's really going on inside. Real diamonds have a shine to them, but they are translucent, not transparent like glass. Broken people are the same – they will generally allow you in so far at first but no more. The reason for this is probably a lack of trust or a sense of shame. There will also be a touch of fear. After all, they've been through some darkness and pressure that we can only imagine – but don't be put off. It just shows that the need is real.

3. Lastly, diamonds are hard, being one of the toughest substances known to man. Looking at life, you have to be prepared for resistance to some degree when setting out to work with people who've been crushed and stressed, because the fact is that their experiences have formed them this way. The key, though, is that they are there – being present is a positive sign.

So, with these things in mind, if you're involved at this point in the process, you can safely know that this person before you is ready to be worked with.

Stage 3: Cleaning

The process of cleaning a real rough diamond is more involved than perhaps you might think, and it involves boiling in acid, as water alone generally won't be able to get out all of the oxides that have been pressed into whatever fine cracks there are over the surface. A cut and polished diamond doesn't take as much cleaning and will usually shine up in a bit of hot water and detergent, but that's for later in the process.

So, don't be alarmed if things begin to get messy during this phase as years of stuff can literally come pouring out. All you have to remember is that healing is taking place. This is a part of the process that most people want to skip if possible, so if you're involved in helping someone else clean out years of faulty mindsets or attitudes or bad or painful experiences – well done! The difficult truth is that if you do skip this part of the process you are, in effect, blocking the potential value of that person.

Because this part of the process is intense it will take commitment to see it through. You need sensitivity (you don't want to add dirt), a listening ear, and you'll need to be accessible and available to answer questions and provide answers wherever possible.

As a Christian, I believe that the word of God plays a significant role in this cleaning process as does prayer, and I've personally found this to be true in my own personal healing and then in helping other hurting people. The Bible has given me a mirror to measure my reality with, along with instructions for living, and prayer has connected me to a source of life that cannot be adequately explained but can be personally known. And the positive "coincidences" from applying these things just grows and grows.

Stage 4: Cutting

This follows on from the cleaning process and is where the real-life transformation begins and can actually be seen to be taking place. I've devoted a chapter to the process for crafting a leader – "The 'Michelangelo Method' (Developing a leader by crafting the 'who')" – and this is where it all begins to actually take shape.

In real diamond terms, after it has been removed from its environment, the external stuff that has clung to the potential diamond has been removed and the cracks have been cleaned, the diamond will be cut. For a person this is where mentoring is crucial, as the best way to cut a diamond is with another diamond.

Contrary to popular misunderstanding, not every diamond goes into a ring or a piece of jewellery – many are used industrially as tools to cut and shape other substances. So, decisions are made as to the diamond's future use. But once it's decided, the cutting begins.

We had a saying where I grew up in the East End of London – "You learn from the cut, not the stitches…!" – and there is much learning that needs to take place during this phase. It can take months or even years depending on how the person being worked with responds to the cut. Many people become discouraged at the time it takes, but encourage them that where God is concerned, He doesn't measure the time – He measures the growth. It's better to go on and finish things than just to start them and leave them undone.

Some things that might need cutting away begin with the obvious such as selfish attitudes and actions, bad habits, distractions – and this can include places or even people that are negative or dangerous to the growth process. These things are hard but necessary and must be handled very sensitively, especially where family units are concerned.

For example, I'm very pro-marriage. I think that good marriages promote a healthy environment for both the couple and any children they might have, so I would never willingly do anything to get in the way of that. But when there's brokenness or addiction or abuse, there may have to be some hard decisions made. I'd never want someone to stay in an abusive relationship where there was a possibility of violence, or an addictive relationship where there was neglect, say, but obviously there are steps to these situations. Remember that butchers use hatchets, but surgeons use scalpels (and diamonds cut diamonds). Be surgical.

It's also helpful to bear in mind that diamonds can be recut if necessary, which means that nothing needs to be permanent. I've experienced this in different ways. Often a wife with an addicted husband will work to get him into a recovery programme, which is great, as long as they are prepared to support them for the whole process (and this is by no means certain). Quite often they begin to feel the real pressure of taking care of business alone and see that their spouse is doing great in the programme – he's clean and positive (but unfinished) – and they want them back prematurely. This is like taking bread out of the oven before it's raised or chicken out of the pot before it's cooked – no good for anyone.

That's just one example and it's what makes this part of the process one of the most challenging, and, paraphrasing G. K. Chesterton, it hasn't been tried and found wanting, it's been found difficult and left untried.

Stage 5: Polishing

When a diamond is cut and shaped, it can then be polished. This is where its facets are defined – those distinct areas that give it it's unique and wonderful shine. In the context of working with people, this takes the form of exposure to different experiences to create the opportunity to develop in different areas of life. Education is one area that can help to polish someone as it challenges thinking patterns, and then there's the exposure to different cultures, with trips to different places to meet new people, who possibly have very different lifestyles, a positive way of enabling this to take place.

I travel extensively and have lived in several different countries for differing periods of time, and it has really helped to shape me. Wherever possible, if I'm going on a short-term trip, I'll take some people with me that I've been working with. It's amazing how exposure to these different arenas can really help to create these new facets in a person's life. Sometimes a trip to a theatre or a restaurant or even a shopping trip to buy new clothes can add something new.

Never assume that everyone you are working with has had the same experiences you've had. Quite often, these things can open up a whole new world of possibility for someone, which in turn will add value to their existence.

This polishing is where confidence in their new state can be reinforced and is too often either overlooked or undervalued. In the Victory Homes my ministry runs we make sure that our residents get new suits or dresses – outfits that help reinforce the new life of dignity that they've been longing for. We help them with their medical or dental maintenance. Just little things like this can go a long way to shining the diamond.

Stage 6: Setting

You want to set up the people you're working with for a "win". This means that you want to get them in the right setting and it's important that you identify where your "diamond" will be most effective. And then you reinforce that – you back it up with everything you've got, and one way is by introducing them to the right people and giving them permission to be themselves. After all, some diamonds fit into the setting of a workshop where they will help to cut other diamonds, or in a drill bit that will cause a breakthrough in some area. But some will be a part of someone's marriage joy, sitting on their finger, while others will adorn something like a necklace or a crown.

If you can take those pictures and utilise them in the lives of the people you have in front of you, it will enable them to fit into their optimum role – but just remember that wherever it is that they are placed, it's ultimately for their benefit and not just for yours.

Stage 7: Presenting

Finally, we come to the time of releasing.

As any parent of a child leaving home can understand, this can be difficult. Some mentors or coaches or guides lose it here. Timing is crucial – if you hold on too long you might lose something valuable. But there's a key thing to know here – your gain is the satisfaction of seeing that person become everything they were created to be… and that in itself should be enough. If you want more than that – well, maybe you yourself need to go back to the cutting room for a bit of reshaping!

But seriously, when you see someone reach a place of fullness of potential and opportunities that they wouldn't normally have had open up for them, and you've played even a small part in that process, the feeling you get just cannot be described – but it can be known. So, start digging!

THE "MICHELANGELO METHOD" (DEVELOPING A LEADER BY CRAFTING THE "WHO")

When you think of a "leader", you probably have a picture in your head of someone who has added all sorts of amazing skills and talents to their lives. And while that's very true, there's something that also happens that many people don't look at or talk about much, and that's the part where the leader grows by having stuff removed.

Some people believe that leaders are born like it, while others are of the opinion that they're formed into it. Both of these ideas contain truth, with the formation of a leader carrying the most weight, but I prefer to think of leaders as being "revealed" – step by step, crafted from a raw material. You begin with something rough and natural and as it is shaped another form emerges, that as a unique thing is actually in itself a masterpiece. In the development of a leader, I've come to look at this as the "Michelangelo method".

Michelangelo di Lodovico Buonarroti Simoni, most commonly known simply as Michelangelo, was a famous Italian artist who, amongst many other works of art, created the statue of a young biblical King David, between ad 1501–1504. Sculpted of Carrara marble and presently located in the Galleria dell 'Accademia in Florence, Italy, it stands to a height of 5.17m (203.5in). That's the height of an average two-storey British house! It's a truly massive thing that in my mind opens up all sorts of parallels with the development of a leader. One of the main reasons for this is a story I once heard about the artist while he was sculpting what was to become his masterpiece. Someone came upon him chiselling at an enormous piece of rock and asked him what he was making, to which he replied, "I'm making a statue of David."

"But Maestro, how do you know what to do?" came the cry from beneath him.

Michelangelo's answer made so much sense – "I just chip away everything that doesn't look like David…"!

This story made some things very clear to me about the development of a person from raw reality into someone whose life has the possibility of influencing others in a truly positive way. And I believe it happens in three stages:

Stage 1: Mining - recognising the masterpiece

In studying scripture through the years I've noticed that the way the creator works is from the inside out, because the external form of something always has more integrity when it flows from the right internal form. Inside everyone is their future and when we put things in the right order of importance, we will achieve the right results.

There are two scriptures that brought this home to me and have informed the way I work with individuals.

The first is found in the book of Proverbs, part of the wisdom literature in the Old Testament:

Train up a child in the way he should go, and when he is old, he will not depart from it.

PROVERBS 22:6 (NKJV)

There are two main parts to this scripture – the first part speaks of "training" and the path a "child" (or in our context, whoever we're working with) should follow. Sometimes, though, more emphasis is placed on the act of "training" without looking at the child's destined path. This is where the one doing the training makes the dangerous mistake of trying to form the person they're working with into their own image. This can then become more like conforming them into a clone than releasing the masterpiece.

While it's very true that all children need to be trained in general areas – good manners, life disciplines, etc. – it's wise to understand that every child is uniquely created to follow a specific path in life. As a result, every child has unique talents, gifts and abilities. It is the responsibility of the parents and other teachers to recognise that path, and then use everything they can to help equip that person to find and follow that path. That's the key, and a different way of translating this verse makes this point even clearer:

Direct your children onto the right path, and when they are older, they will not leave it.

PROVERBS 22:6 (NLT)

This first principle leads on to the second part of the scripture because when this is done, it is more likely that the person will follow that path for the rest of their life because it's in them to do that. If you can recognise the real picture contained within that person, then you can help it to develop into the future masterpiece that will retain its value into the future.

The second scripture that hammers this home is found in Paul's Roman letter:

And do not be conformed to this world, but be transformed by the renewing of your mind, that you may prove what is that good and acceptable and perfect will of God.

ROMANS 12:2 (NKJV)

The first idea is that conformity – being pressured into shape – by external forces into an image that's not what was intended for you is warned against. Far too many people have accepted a life that, whilst being conformed on the outside and looking good, is actually stripping them of the joy of living. This is one of the root causes of escapism in its many manifestations, because the reality of the life they were created to live is crushed and deformed and then the life they have found themselves living is crushed and begins the slow process of decay.

But there is good news for someone trapped in that slow death. They can be transformed by having their thought processes changed. The word "transformed" is such a powerful one when leading broken people because it gives a real hope of lasting change. The concept is that of a literal metamorphosis – a shape-shift – from one form into another, and if we can see the real picture of a person's destiny, we can begin to guide them on their journey of revelation.

Stage 2: Defining – removing the unnecessary

Secondly, and most painfully, our onward growth really begins to happen as certain areas of our lives are removed. This seems to be the opposite of what we would think would happen. Surely, to develop in life you need to add things? Although eventually that does become true and a real necessity, it's only when those things that are, in reality, stopping you from developing are first taken away that anything of value can be added. I've seen this take place over and over, and I've experienced this cutting away many times in my own journey, and as this takes place in the life of the person you are helping to develop, something wonderful is literally revealed. It's like unwrapping a surprise gift – you know something good is contained inside but you can't fully see what it is until its shape is fully unveiled. This takes careful handling, and patience is a real virtue during this stage as the delicate act of removing becomes the excitement of revealing. Too much at once could cause a collapse, whilst too little can prolong the pain of the process, and one of the main things that I've come to recognise that needs to be chipped away in order for the people we work with to become everything they were created to become is the one thing everyone tries to naturally protect as much as possible – because it's yourself...

Selfish pride and self-reliance

Biblically, this is one of the original desires of humanity that has caused so many problems throughout its history. It includes everything that has to do with thinking you are the centre of the universe, including selfish attitudes and mindsets.

I'm a creationist by persuasion; I believe that everything came from someone – an intelligent, personal being who we call God. This being identifies Himself in Biblical scripture as "YWHW" – "I Am" – which means He exists eternally and is the "uncaused first cause" with no beginning or end. Of course, not everyone believes this and many people theorise about alternative causes of matter and life – and none of these "beliefs" can be proved empirically, including Christianity. People who believe in the Bible as being God's revealed word understand by faith which hangs upon certain "evidences" that it was this being who created all things and also keeps all things working together in the universe He created through His son, Jesus Christ.

But there came a point when the first humans mentioned in the Bible – Adam and Eve – were tempted to take things into their own hands, or in essence to become the gods of their own lives. This was really unnecessary because they already had everything they needed for peace and purpose in life given to them by the creator God to take care of – but for some reason it wasn't enough! The autonomous control over what they did and the direction in which they would live their lives became more important than just living in gratitude for what they had received. Fast-forward to our day and we see this as being something that is recommended as an essential human right – but the majority of people simply don't know how to handle being a "god", and when this self-reliance is taken to the extreme of becoming selfish pride, it in turn becomes destructive.

The opposite of this is, of course, humility, and this is not a reality that everyone truly understands. It's not as much about thinking you're less than you are as it is about realising who you really are and where you actually fit in life. When this happens, a person becomes less independent and more interdependent. This is probably the biggest cut that someone will face, but it's essential for the true shape of a person to be revealed.

You might be thinking, "How do I facilitate this cutting business when I'm helping another person?" The answer to this question is that the responsibility for the final form is not yours – it's God's. He's the maestro and that person is His masterpiece – we are simply His apprentices. We do our best to position the person at His direction and the maestro then uses the tools of time and circumstances – as well as His revealed will contained in the words of the Bible – to chip away at the unnecessary stuff.

But while God does the real work, don't underestimate the responsibility He gives to us to make sure the positioning is done accurately and at the right time. Putting someone in the wrong position at the wrong time can cause something to be added when it should in fact be removed – or vice versa – and even worse can happen when the leader forgets he's an apprentice and starts to think he's the maestro and starts chopping away using his own methods. Then he can be actually creating a monster in his own image, rather than the image that the real maestro (God) has in mind.

However, when we, the apprentice leaders, listen and obey God's directions, we enable the person we're working with to take the right shape in the right order. I've seen this happen over and over again.

One young man I worked with is called Anton. Anton was born and raised in Trafford, Manchester and while growing up became entangled in the gang life of the streets.

When I first met Anton, he gave me a brief overview of his past and then a rundown of his achievements and desires. He then basically told me how he was to be placed and what he should be doing. That happens a lot with people who think they're free but haven't actually defined what was holding them bound. Anton was not outwardly "messed up"; he looked the part and was even connected spiritually, but there was something still missing on the inside and so his life wasn't actually working in the way it should, a bit like that mobile phone that looks intact and has a signal but is stuck so that it can't be used.

The problem was he wasn't fully developed. Much of his potential character was still undefined and embedded in the stone of his past life and experiences. If you can imagine a human form being sculpted from a block of marble with only the top part being revealed in a rough form, then that's what Anton looked like telling me these things. Just because someone's head has been freed and their eyes and mouth work, it doesn't mean they know what they're seeing or talking about. The potential for his life was big and obviously there, but the actual ability to operate in that potential was still mostly stuck in that old slab of stone. It would take some more time and a few necessary challenges for his full form to be carved out. Thankfully, Anton took the cutting process seriously and has overcome everything that's come his way spiritually, emotionally, relationally and practically, and is currently a businessman who specialises in mentoring others. But he had to cooperate in the process without cracking.

There is something I've seen over and over when leading people from a place of brokenness – the tendency for them to run ahead of the process because they have had a bit of a breakthrough in a couple of areas of their lives, without developing a more complete and mature form.

The truth is there's no shortcut to the cutting edge.

Most artists I've spoken to define the entire form of their subject, even roughly, before they begin to refine it, because there is more economy of effort that way. After all, there's no point in having a half-perfect masterpiece, is there? Imagine Da Vinci's *Mona Lisa* with half a face, just the one eye following you everywhere in the room…

But the temptation when working with someone you're helping to develop is to release them unfinished into the public sphere. In Christian ministry I've seen couples being released to start – or take over – churches, that are still entangled with past issues or haven't fully developed their own relationship before they enter the war zone. Sometimes roles or expectations haven't been defined which can be a ticking time bomb if not caught and addressed in time. The problem is that elevation in any area always comes with an added weight of responsibility and that will expose any faults in the foundation, so at least you need a whole outline before you can move the process forward.

When this stage is properly completed, you'll have before you a rough outline of the person as they were destined to look. You can recognise their shape, but they're by no means the finished article. Something has been defined – but now it gets refined.

Stage 3: Refining - adding the detail

Secondly, once the desired form has been revealed in the life of someone you're working with, you then need to refine it. On Michelangelo's statue of David, I can imagine him taking time to add detail to the eyes and nose and the shape of the muscles. There are practical ways that this can be achieved, through the setting of tasks and by spending some quality time evaluating and talking things through, and if you're committed to seeing this work through, the results in the life of the person you're working with can be stunning – literally a work of art.

This process will take time and care to get the most out of that original rough block of potential leader that you are working with, and that's okay – but most of all it takes vision. Think of it more as art backed up by science than just using a formula, and you'll also have more enjoyment in doing it over and over again, as each person you work with in this way develops their own shape as well as being shaped into the masterpiece that they will become. The apostle Paul, writing to the church in Ephesus, in Asia, tells them:

For we are God's masterpiece. He has created us anew in Christ Jesus, so we can do the good things he planned for us long ago.

EPHESIANS 2:10 (NLT)

This is how the creator of the universe works in our lives, and I believe it's how He wants us to work with others too. But it's not just a casual thing. It takes thought and planning and a desire to understand.

Have you ever looked at or studied a masterpiece? Some of the best of them are infused with good science. If you look at the works of another famous master, Leonardo Da Vinci, you will see how mathematics and geometry and other scientific methods are used throughout, and in fact are essential to the process of creating these works of art, so it should, therefore, come as no surprise that there are certain essentials that are needed when helping a leader to form. Those instinctive flourishes that flow from the hand of the sculptor are guided by an understanding of both the anatomical form that's being revealed as well as the techniques required to bring it about, and just as Michelangelo's statue of David was based on a recognisable human form, so I believe we have a form to follow also – Jesus of Nazareth.

It's been my experience to undergo increasing revelation as I submit my life to the hand of the master. It's working for me, so I pray it'll work for you too.

THE LEADERSHIP OUTCOME

The reality is that working with broken people is hard. Leading them from a broken history to a fulfilling destiny can be even more challenging. But if you can see the process through its phases, the possibility is that you can end up with a former broken person beginning their own journey of leading broken people. That's been my experience and I've seen it successfully reproduce in the lives of other people, and this is one of the outcomes we look for.

Not everyone you work with will become a "leader" in practice – hopefully some will – but I'm of the opinion that everyone can be taught about this subject so that they will at least have an appreciation for it.

Some people think that leaders are born that way – and some possibly are born with leadership gifts within them – but most either have it thrust on them, or at some stage in their life determine to learn how to lead. I've come to the understanding that leaders can be developed and that there's a process to becoming a person of influence, as well as a price, and the fact is that many simply don't want to pay the price or allow themselves to be developed. It's no surprise, then, how confusing the subject can become with so many people seeking to define it.

I once heard someone say that, "Any fool can learn from their own mistakes, but a wise man learns from the mistakes of others".

So, this chapter has three things for you to consider:

Firstly, we need to look at what leadership is – in a nutshell and very practically – and what types of leaders there are at a basic level. This includes what I've identified as three unique, main power spots that you'll come across when starting out on the journey as a leader, and these give permission for people to begin to think like a leader without having their heads fall off because of all the technicalities.

Then, secondly, we'll look at some practical grown-up reality stuff about leadership. I don't for one minute imagine it to be an all-encompassing study, but I'm hoping it'll be enough to give you a little bit of wisdom to be going on with.

So, what types of leaders are there? And what is leadership? These are the two big questions to answer, and the answers are both simpler than you think and yet more involved than you'd like.

1) The leader - being

Most leadership "experts" agree that it has at its core the fact of "influence". The author John Maxwell famously used this term to explain its function, but he wasn't the only one. Peter G. Northouse's excellent book entitled *Leadership* also speaks of a leader utilising influence as part of the process where people are enabled to reach a common goal (paraphrase).

This makes it clear that actual leadership is more than just doing something first – or even reaching somewhere before others. That just makes you a front runner or even a scout for others. But true leadership utilises its skills for joint outcomes.

Another interesting concept is that of "good" and "bad" leadership. If the focus is purely on mobilising people towards an outcome, then it could be said that Adolf Hitler, the leader of Nazi Germany and architect of the Second World War, or the communist leaders Stalin or Mao Zedong, or even going further back in history, Attila the Hun, could be termed "good leaders". After all, they were good at it! They influenced and mobilised whole people groups. But I don't think that's how leadership should necessarily be gauged.

In my Leadership MA studies, I came across this concept of "good leadership" being defined as "not just good leadership" but "leadership for good". My unit instructor, Richard Tiplady, PhD, made the point that the motive for influencing people is crucial to whatever it accomplishes. I agree with that idea and I think that losing sight of this principle can divert leadership from positive and healthy to negative and unhealthy.

With this in mind, think about "why" you want to lead. If it's for personal gain, then leading broken people is probably not for you. I've seen people get involved in this work because they see an opening for profit and they're more interested in the income than the outcome. Sadly, the "commodity" involved are human lives and it can become destructive if that understanding gets lost or overlooked for the sake of financial gain.

On the other hand, if your motive is to have loads of grateful people shouting your name then you'll probably enjoy it for a while. After all, you're their saviour, right? There's incredible danger in this motive, however, because all you'll create will be clones of yourself who will one day decide they no longer need you and you'll be dropped like a piece of garbage. I've seen this happen and it's unhealthy for everyone involved. In my mind there's only one saviour and that's Jesus Christ – but even if that's not your personal conviction, don't fall into this ego trap.

So, what should be the motive? Is there a right one? I believe there is and it's simply that you should want to lead broken people out of their situation because *it's the right thing to do*. The outcome is that they will be in a better place and that benefits the world we live in.

Leadership beginnings

There are many leadership types and definitely too many to look at in one chapter of this book, but I've identified three unique entry-level power spots that can certainly help the people you're working with. These are very basic and can – and should – be developed and expanded as one gains more experience and learning, but I've found these useful when helping people beginning their leadership journeys to identify their starting points.

They are:

- Caregivers
- Managers
- Visionaries

Let's drill down on these a bit.

The caregiver

These are basically carers of people. They have this emphasis in whatever area of life and work they find themselves in. They include these traits:

- Caring
- Listeners
- Counsellors
- Connectors
- True lovers of people
- Always available to spend time with people
- Encouragers and builders of people
- People-oriented

These are the type of leaders who can be relied upon to take care of people all the time. People are their calling, their vocation and their primary focus. They'll visit and talk on the phone and listen for hours. Not everyone can naturally do this, and we need these types of leaders on the shop floor of any venture we have because this is often where nuts and bolts changes occur. If this describes you then well done! It's a beautiful thing to have this as your heart motivation as an influencer and if you identify these traits in the life of someone you're working with then give it the permission it needs to fly.

The manager

These are the administrators. Without this type of leader everything would grind to a halt. They enable help to become more effective as it becomes more efficient. They are:

- Educators
- Managers
- Implementors
- Maintainers or "follow-uppers"
- Organisational
- Detail lovers
- Finishers
- Task-oriented

We see a difference here in that they are outwardly not as focused on people. But don't let that distract you from the fact that even though their skill set is different to the caregiver, their motives are for the good of those same people. These types of leaders are essential to make sure that the right things happen in the right way. If this describes you then you are crucial to the work of helping people. I've seen people I'm working with struggle with caring for people in the way the caregiver does, but then come alive when there's detailing to be done for them. Encourage this as it's an amazing and often overlooked part of leadership. When teamed up with caregivers, real change becomes the norm.

The visionary

These are the inspirational ones – the seers of things beyond the horizon. These are important because they are directionally and strategically minded. This group are:

- Visionaries
- Communicators
- Ideas people
- Front runners
- Inspirational
- Struggle with detail
- Starters
- Goal-oriented

Imagine a group of people traveling through a deep, dark forest. The caregivers are making sure that everyone is doing fine. The managers are making sure that every need is provided for. But the visionary is at the top of a tree, having climbed up there, and after looking around shouts down to the others, "You're going in the wrong direction!" I know it's humorous, but if there are no visionary leaders it can sometimes mean that broken people can be well cared for and maintained but not go too far. If this is where you fit, then don't worry too much about your lack of admin skills or even your lack of ability to listen to people for hours, just keep looking forward.

When I'm working with a group of upcoming leaders, I'll present these types to them and ask them to identify with one of them. Then I'll divide the group into three with each group being one of the leadership types discussed. This does two things:

It gives them permission to be themselves and not have to conform to a pre-set mould. They can see that others are like them, and it's okay.

Then, secondly, they can look at the other groups and understand that not everyone identifies with the same characteristics, and because of that they can begin to see and understand that teams work better than individuals because nobody has everything that's going to be needed.

By all means, grow your skills in every area, but be comfortable knowing there's probably one area you flow in better than others. And if you do that then look for and empower that in the lives of the people you're working with.

I personally flow best as a visionary type. I enjoy seeing possibilities and getting things started. I've had to learn the other skills to some degree as my own leadership journey has developed, but I always default back to being a visionary, so I've come to look for and appreciate leaders that function differently to me. I need them, and they need me. You'll be happy to know that broken people I've worked with throughout the years have become key leaders in their own right on my staff and in our network of churches. Their primary gifts are different, but their motivations are the same. They have taken on their challenges and grown influence and now use it to help broken and hurting people to achieve the same outcomes they have realised

Before we move on, though, there are some non-negotiable qualities that I believe good leaders must have. Once again, there are lots of books which look at these areas in much more detail, but I feel I should mention at least a few of my top ones here. These are not in order but without them the leader will possibly become out of order.

There's "character", which is what you look like when no one else is looking at you. Sometimes this can be confused with "charisma", which is your giftedness. When this misunderstanding occurs something bad will usually follow. This goes back to the "good leadership" or "leadership for good" point we looked at earlier. A good leader needs to be gifted in the right areas, but more importantly needs to be doing things in the right way for the right reason.

What about "humility"? In some leadership cultures that's not spoken about because there's a misconception that the leader needs to be "the person of power for the hour", but that can just be a cover for pride. I believe leaders need to be decisive, but also need to know when and where others can be more effective than they are. Humility understands its limits whilst remaining secure in its position, and a humble leader will be able to empower others to grow at the right time in the right way without losing influence. This creates a more effective and efficient system.

Then there's the question of "integrity", which basically means that you're complete or undivided. There's nothing worse than a leader who is falling apart or is double-minded. Having integrity also means you can be trusted. This is incredibly important as most people – especially broken people – don't care how "incredible" the things you can do are if you're not "credible" as a person.

All these elements make up a leader's "human capital", or in other words the things that qualify them to "be" a person that others will follow. But how to "do" leadership stuff is sometimes a subject that can be overlooked. This is the "social capital" side of things and is in essence the difference between being a "leader" and someone who actively engages in the work of "leadership".

2) The leadership - doing

I think it's probable that everyone who has a dream of engaging in this type of work has experienced that dream becoming a nightmare at least once. Because the truth is that some people are nightmares! For a start, not everyone wants to change. Then others do want to change but take a lot longer for their selfish kung fu grip on the things that are destroying them to be released. Knowing these things and what follows can help you to set up strong leadership boundaries, which will not only guard your sanity, but will enable the people you're working with to find their own path forwards.

I've been in some type of leadership since 1996. At first, I think I got these concepts backwards in that I'd do leadership stuff before my character had been crafted into a leader worth following. I'm grateful that I had the room to learn and here's some of my hard-learned leadership keys:

Always keep the main thing the main thing

Try to remember "why" you do what you do. Do your best not to get distracted with side issues. Paul the apostle told Timothy, the young man he was training:

> *No soldier gets entangled in civilian pursuits, since his aim is to please the one who enlisted him.*

2 TIMOTHY 2:4 (ESV)

Whenever you drift away from your "why", your leadership can even morph into something else. Being a leader is a high calling and involves acts of "service". I've seen some leaders lose sight of this as they begin to focus more on the perceived "perks" of their position rather than the actual "works" of their position. If you start doing it for the "income" rather than the "outcome", you're venturing into sticky ground.

This servant-hearted mentality is essential if you want your leadership to be "transformational" and not just "transactional".

Transformational leadership is a concept whereby the leader is able to inspire their followers to work towards common organisational goals. Where this happens, followers will change and increase their expectations, perceptions, and motivations, and in doing so will see effective change. These leaders engage with their followers and actively encourage them, through a communicated vision of future possibility, to achieve greater outcomes.

Transactional leadership is different in that it places more emphasis on punishments and rewards for behaviour. Transactional leaders focus more on compliance from their followers to rules and structures. It's a bit like the "carrot and stick" style of leadership. My problem with this is that it is great at maintaining the status quo, but not so good at building people to become agents of change.

Both of these styles have a place, but if we're going to stay on target to lead broken people into their destiny, we should be aiming for the people we work with to become catalysts in their own right – because transformed people transform things.

Understand - not everyone is going to like you

It doesn't matter how lovely you are or how much you want to help other people – there will always be people who don't like you.

Sometimes it's because of ignorance – people don't know the real you and possibly can't or won't take the time to get to know you. So, they make negative assumptions about you. Mainly it's because of insecurity – they feel threatened by you because you can either do what they can't, or you expose their inadequacies. Whatever the reason, it'll happen from time to time.

You'll come across chronic cynics who never fully invest into other people but always stand on the side-lines and critique everyone else.

Then there are those people who are just hurting – and hurting people hurt people. At times, people will bleed over you, even though it wasn't you who cut them.

But however it happens and whoever it is, your place is to love them, guide them and pour vision into them, but don't be surprised if they take what you've given and then choose to move on. At least let them leave knowing you have done what you can for them.

Remember this – when someone does or says something bad to you and you respond with patience and love, you're giving them an opportunity to see how they could have acted.

As a leader, your wellbeing is in your hands - not someone else's

Don't expect other people to be looking out for you or noticing all your needs or taking care of you, because you'll be waiting a long time. Other people can help in some areas, but you have to look after the health of your own heart and mind.

You will give time, energy and emotion to people, and at times, they will trample it like it means nothing. Good leadership is not about working out ways to prevent this but figuring out ways to learn how to deal with it in a way that is healthy.

Resentment and emotional insecurity can cause you to harden your heart more quickly than you realise, which will leave you untrusting and unavailable to others, and this can knock you off track very easily. The hard truth is that when you're leading broken people you will have to learn how to be betrayed, but not destroyed. Don't hold it all to yourself – talk about it to the right people at the right time. This is where it's always better to be insulated than isolated. The people you are leading, though, are not the best people to crumble in front of. Make sure you have a good support network of like-minded people who are operating on the same level as you. They can usually understand your struggles because they've walked in your shoes. I was told not to seek to make acquaintances, but to make allies – people with a similar nature and purpose – and I'm glad I managed to do that. These friends and mentors have been invaluable to me and yours will be to you also.

Leadership is always a two-way street

In leadership, everybody around you is someone who needs something from you, and the thing is, you also you need something from them. They will need your wisdom and guidance, your support, your emotional and spiritual capacity, your consistency and your vision for the future. You will need their willingness to follow where you lead and to do what needs to be done. Those two dynamics often find themselves in great tension.

So as a leader it helps to know the 3 As of mobilisation. These are:

- **Acceptance** – where people follow your leadership without protest. This is where they decide to trust what you're suggesting because you've made your case well.
- **Agreement** – is where they agree with the direction you propose and start moving towards a goal you've set.
- **Alignment** – which is where they start fully cooperating with the process and you can start building the momentum necessary to make the change work.

Building this consensus is where your credibility really comes home, and this is what "social capital" is all about, because at its core, influence involves trust. When this operates in a healthy way your influence will be effective.

It takes time to build it right

There's no shortcut to the cutting edge. People are different, and some take longer than others to catch what you're giving to them. Some need fixing while others need filling. The question that mature leaders ask goes like, "Is this right or wrong?" On the other hand, immaturity asks, "Is this hard or easy?" The thing is, though, easy might look quicker but that's not necessarily the truth. More often than not, easy takes you on a route of distraction and that is the enemy of direction. So always do what's right, because only progress that's heading in the right direction is good – even if it takes a bit longer.

When you prioritise quality over quantity, your work will gain a momentum which will see you enjoy both if you just keep doing what is right.

Learn to be flexible

Some people are so stiff and controlling that they become inflexible. Don't be like that! Remember this – "Blessed are the flexible for they shall not be bent out of shape". I once went to join a yoga class. The young instructor asked me, "So, how flexible are you?" I replied, "I can't make Wednesdays or Fridays." Hopefully you at least groaned. But the point is that your idea of flexibility might be different to the people you're working with. Learn to adapt and overcome and remember that some things are "STC" – "subject to change".

It's important to plan and be strategic and to dream big dreams, but hold them like you would a bar of soap – with an open hand; too much force and it'll shoot out of your grasp, but when your grip is flexible you can guide and not control.

Get ready for surprises

Those you expect the most from will possibly let you down the most, and those you don't expect much from will possibly exceed your expectations. Some people from my early days tell me they never expected much from me – a former criminal and drug addict. They were surprised! I've been surprised more times than I can count. I've worked with people with so much potential who just fail. Sometimes it seems there's no rhyme or reason to it. But I've also worked with people who outdo all your expectations, and when that happens it starts a whole new possibility of change.

So, be a leader and do leadership in a way that helps other people to become everything they were created to be. It's not only possible, it's necessary. Broken people can be fixed, and when they are up and running, they can become the biggest source of help the world will ever see. Play your part and let God do the rest.

Brokenness is everywhere. People are valuable and you can make a difference. So, if you really want to help, just do what you can do… You won't regret it.